THE NORTH CAROLINA CHAIN GANG

PATTERSON SMITH REPRINT SERIES IN
CRIMINOLOGY, LAW ENFORCEMENT, AND SOCIAL PROBLEMS

I. A County Convict Road Camp

II. A County Convict Road Camp

In this picture the tarpaulin is lowered to protect against the weather.

PUBLICATION NO. 39: PATTERSON SMITH REPRINT SERIES IN
CRIMINOLOGY, LAW ENFORCEMENT, AND SOCIAL PROBLEMS

THE NORTH CAROLINA CHAIN GANG

A STUDY OF COUNTY CONVICT ROAD WORK

By

JESSE F. STEINER
*Professor of Social Technology in the
University of North Carolina*

and

ROY M. BROWN
*Research Associate in the Institute for Research
in Social Science at the University
of North Carolina*

HV
8929
N72
S7
1969

135223

Montclair, New Jersey

PATTERSON SMITH

1969

SBN 87585-039-1

Library of Congress Catalog Card Number: 69-14949

PREFACE

In October, 1925, the Institute for Research in Social Science of the University of North Carolina entered upon an investigation of Negro crime in the state as a part of a larger study of the Negro in the South. Since a study of this nature is closely bound up with the entire criminal situation, the scope of this investigation was broadened until it assumed the form of a state-wide survey of crime which will include such factors as the nature and amount of crime, the conditions under which crime is produced, the cost of crime, case histories of criminals, the administration of criminal justice, methods of penal treatment, and crime prevention. This investigation, unlike the usual crime survey, was not planned as an intensive study to be completed in a given period of time, but rather as a continuous search for facts persisted in year after year so that there may be in the files of the Institute for Research in Social Science the most complete and authoritative information possible concerning the state crime problem. From time to time monographs dealing with different phases of this subject will be published either by the University Press or issued as bulletins in coöperation with the State Board of Charities and Public Welfare. This volume is the first to appear in this series of crime studies and will be followed by additional volumes as soon as the material is ready for publication.

Limitation in resources, both of personnel and of financial support, has made it impracticable to embark from the beginning upon a well balanced program of investigation covering all the phases of the subject above mentioned. At the present time, the personnel engaged in this study comprise a Director and five assistants. Of these latter, one is a research associate, two are research assistants, and two are graduate students. Among the topics to which attention has first been directed are a statistical analysis of superior court records, a similar study of recorders' courts, the administrative costs of crime, case histories of Negro criminals, and the county chain gang system. Plans are already under way for a study of criminal justice including police administration and criminal court procedure, the after careers of persons discharged from state and county prisons, and the problem of juvenile delinquency.

In the preparation of this volume, valuable assistance was given by Mr. Lee M. Brooks and Mr. Arthur F. Raper, both research assistants in the Institute for Research in Social Science, who contributed the chapters on the economic aspects of county convict road work and case histories of Negro criminals. Special thanks are due Mrs. Kate Burr Johnson, State Commissioner of Public Welfare, for permission to use material in the files of her Department. Mention should also be made of Mr. R. Eugene Brown, a member of the staff of the State Board of Charities and Public Welfare, and Mr. L. G. Whitley, Inspector of Penal Institutions, who furnished valuable information gained by their official contact with the county chain gang system. Finally grateful acknowledgment should be made of the cordial coöperation of county superintendents of public welfare and other county officials in this investigation of county convict road work throughout the state.

CHAPEL HILL, N. C.
  JANUARY, 1927

J. F. S.
R. M. B.

CONTENTS

ILLUSTRATIONS

THE NORTH CAROLINA CHAIN GANG

Chapter I

THE COUNTY CONVICT CHAIN GANG AS
A PENAL INSTITUTION

IN THE history of American penal methods, the county convict chain gang system stands out as an interesting attempt to solve the problem of prison labor. Overshadowed as it has been by the state prisons with their elaborate buildings and varied industries, this extensive experiment in the use of unselected groups of county prisoners for road construction and maintenance has failed to attract the attention it deserves. The standard texts on penology have given it only passing mention and the public in general has not realized the extent and significance of this utilization of convict labor in the interest of the good roads movement.

While the convict chain gang system is now limited almost entirely to the Southern states, it was not in origin a distinctively Southern institution. During the last quarter of the 19th century there seems to have been a widespread feeling favorable to the employment of convict labor in highway construction, and state laws were passed in various sections of the country authorizing the use of ball and chain on convicts engaged in road work. These laws, revised somewhat, in many instances have been retained, so that specific legal provision for the working of county convicts on the public highways existed as late as 1923 in all the

states of the Union except Rhode Island. [1]   In spite
of this legal basis for the establishment of county
convict road work, this form of penal treatment
never became widely used in the Northern and
Western states.   Large industrial prisons enclosed
behind strong walls became the accepted places of
punishment with a growing tendency to use the
roads and penal farms for selected groups of honor
prisoners.

In the South, however, climatic factors as well as
the general economic situation caused convict road
work to grow in popular favor until it became one
of the major methods of punishing criminals.   The
county chain gang with its armed guards and
prisoners in stripes is still a familiar sight on the
highways of the majority of the Southern states.
In two of these states, Virginia and Maryland, the
convicts assigned to road work are under state
rather than county supervision. Florida until very
recently has followed the plan of leasing county
prisoners to private contractors instead of working
them on the roads under the direction of the county
authorities.   In Louisiana, only eleven of the sixty-
four parishes of that state maintained chain gangs
in 1925.   The State Road Commission of West
Virginia reports that not more than 25 per cent of
the counties in that state work their convicts on the
roads and that only 2 or 3 of these maintain road
camps throughout the whole year.   But in spite of
these exceptions to the prevailing method of handling county prisoners, the county chain gang still
maintains its supremacy as a penal institution in
the South.

[1]U. S. Bureau of Labor Statistics, *Bulletin* 372, pp. 169-265.

In North Carolina, for example, the population of the county convict road camps is almost double that of the state prison. [2] If the comparison is made on the basis of the number of commitments during the year, the prisoners sent to the county camps outnumber those sent to the state prison by more than 10 to 1. While many of the county chain gang prisoners have been convicted of minor offenses, the law permits commitment to labor on the county roads up to a maximum of ten years, and some county convicts are serving long sentences for such serious offenses as rape, burglary, assault with intent to kill, and manslaughter. During the three year period ending June 30, 1925, 48 per cent of those convicted by the Superior Courts of the state were committed to the county chain gangs and only 8 per cent received a sentence to the state prison. It is usually left to the discretion of the presiding judge to determine whether the prisoner convicted of a felony should be sent to the state prison or to the county roads. In some cases local laws specifically provide that prisoners physically unable to work on the roads may be sentenced to the state prison or to the county jail. It is commonly asserted by the state prison officials that those unfit for hard labor are committed to their institution while the strong and able-bodied are required to work out their sentences on the country roads. Whether or not this is true, it is quite obvious that the wider choice of industries in the state prison makes it possible for that institu-

[2]The inmates of the state prison numbered 1,490 on September 30, 1926. At that time the approximate population of the county convict camps was 2,500.

tion to utilize more satisfactorily the labor of different types of prisoners. Another factor which may influence the judge in passing sentence is the general feeling that commitment to the county chain gang is more disgraceful and humiliating than a sentence to the state prison.

Without doubt the motive underlying the establishment and the continuance of the county chain gang is primarily economic. An institution of this kind is admirably suited to provide labor for the short term prisoner who ordinarily would lie idle in the county jail and contribute nothing to his own support. Furthermore this system offers to the county an apparent source of profit in the form of cheap labor for use in the building and maintenance of roads. The average county official in charge of such prisoners thinks far more of exploiting their labor in the interest of good roads, than of any corrective or reformatory value in such methods of penal treatment. When a county has once adopted the plan of convict road work, it becomes necessary to maintain a convict road force sufficient in number to justify the overhead charges for equipment and supervision. Under such circumstances the local criminal courts tend to be looked upon as feeders for the chain gang, and there is evidence in some instances that the mill of criminal justice grinds more industriously when the convict road force needs new recruits.

During the past few years the economic value of county convict road work has been seriously questioned by many county officials as well as by the general public. It is quite probable that if the counties maintaining chain gangs could be induced to keep accurate financial records including unit costs of road construction by convict labor, there would very soon be few county chain gangs. In a recent communication, Ellison Capers, Secretary of the Board of Public Welfare in South Carolina, writes: "The Board of Public Welfare is looking towards the abolition of the chain gang system in South Carolina. Wherever we have had the full coöperation of the county supervisor and the board of county commissioners, in so far as the adequate keeping of records is concerned, it has been proven conclusively that the chain gang system is an economic loss; and it is by these means rather than from a humanitarian standpoint that we are attempting to have the system done away with in our State."

The lack of adequate record keeping by the county authorities in North Carolina has proved to be an almost insuperable obstacle to a satisfactory investigation of this important phase of the chain gang system. In the chapter dealing with this subject, the available evidence is presented which seems to indicate that county convict road work apart from the honor system rests upon a very insecure economic foundation.

The distinguishing feature of the county convict chain gang system as it has been developed in North Carolina and in most of the Southern states, is the plan of working on the public highways an unselected group of prisoners comprising a greater or less number of untrustworthy and desperate men who must be continuously and closely guarded. The honor men in any one camp are frequently limited to those whose duties as cook or truck driver necessitate a considerable amount of freedom. It is assumed that the remainder are "gun men" who must always be under the close supervision of armed guards with authority to shoot to kill, if necessary in order to prevent escapes. Stripes, chains, and shackles are other devices used by the convict camp superintendents to keep such prisoners securely.

This system of penal treatment is frequently criticized on the ground that the use of chains and stripes in public places is unduly humiliating to the prisoners as well as degrading to those who are forced to witness such a spectacle when passing along the highways. This conviction has been strengthened during the past few years by the unfavorable publicity given the chain gang because of the cruel treatment of the convicts in some of the county camps in North Carolina and other Southern states. While these charges of cruelty have thus far been limited to a small minority of the convict camps, it is apparent that the system lends itself readily to such abuses with no adequate means of safeguarding the rights of prisoners. Whenever convicts not under the honor system live and work outside of prison walls, where they face many opportunities for escape, it is easy for those in charge to assume that harsh measures of restraint must be employed in the maintenance of discipline. This is especially true in a county system of administration where there is only a minimum of supervision by the state authorities.

In fact, the most serious problems of management of county chain gangs grow out of this small unit of administration which makes it impracticable to provide proper equipment or place trained personnel in charge.   A board of county commissioners elected by the voters to have general supervision of the county government or a road commission chosen because its members are supposed to be fitted to direct a program of road building find themselves confronted with the problems of a penal system that would challenge the knowledge and skill of experienced prison administrators. The small number of prisoners prevents their proper classification even if means were available for giving them the thorough examination necessary for this purpose.   Since the public demands that the convict road work be operated at the lowest possible cost, the employment of a competent staff of high grade guards is out of the question.   Provision must be made to transport the prisoners considerable distances each day to and from their work, or temporary camps must be constructed and moved from place to place as the occasion demands. The problem of sanitation in the poorly constructed, temporary camps is exceedingly hard to handle.   The matter of discipline becomes especially troublesome when an unassorted group of prisoners is forced to live in cramped and insecure quarters by night and work out in the open by day. Since the majority of the prisoners are worked under the gun, they must remain in compact groups, which often interferes with the economical use of their labor.   These and various other serious problems of administration form an inevitable part of the chain gang system and their solution is frequently far beyond the capacity of the type of men placed in charge.   Their chief responsibility, as they see it, is to keep the prisoners at work and to prevent escapes. No thought is given to the education of the illiterate or to the reformation of those not yet hardened to crime. The chain gang, from their point of view, has no further purpose than to punish criminals through the exploitation of their labor for the public good.

In the following chapters an attempt is made to set forth in detail the history of this penal institution in North Carolina and to discuss in a frank and objective manner the facts concerning its present administration. On the whole, it is a discouraging picture that is presented, for there is evidence on every hand of its mismanagement, inhumanity, and futility. Nevertheless, it is a story of great interest to which students of the prison problem have not given adequate attention.

Chapter 11

EARLY DEVELOPMENT OF THE COUNTY CHAIN GANG SYSTEM

PRIOR to the Civil War there were comparatively few prisoners in North Carolina. There was no state prison. The only prisons for the punishment of offenders were the common jails of the counties. There was no provision for employing prisoners at any sort of labor except that in certain cases the free Negro might be hired out to pay fines and costs. The advisability of the establishment of a state penitentiary had begun to be discussed by the state legislature as early as 1816. In 1846 the proposition of establishing such a state prison had been submitted to a vote of the people and they had voted against it. Instead of imprisonment there were the pillory and the whipping post and even the branding iron, while the death penalty was inflicted for many offenses which are now punished by imprisonment. The Revised Code of 1855, the last codification of laws prior to the Civil War, enumerates as many as seventeen offenses for which the death penalty might be inflicted. Bigamy was punished by branding with a hot iron the letter B upon the cheek. For manslaughter, if the first offense, an M was burned upon the "brawn of the left thumb." In case of perjury in connection with a capital offense, the law required that "the offender shall, instead of the public whipping, have his right ear cut off and severed entirely from his head, and nailed to the pillory by the sheriff, there to remain until sundown." For fifteen offenses the punishment was confinement in the pillory or whipping or both, often supplemented by a fine or imprisonment. Quite frequently the law prescribed that the whipping should be done publicly. A popular sentence of this kind was "thirty-nine lashes on the bare back." In some cases whipping was prescribed for the free Negro when a fine was deemed sufficient punishment for the white man guilty of the same offense.

Specific terms of imprisonment were prescribed for twenty-two offenses. These terms were usually short. In only four cases were the prison terms more than one year and in a fifth the law reads "not less than one year." The longest term of imprisonment prescribed was three years, except that in case of injury to railroads, plank roads, turnpikes, or canals, the offender who was unable to "find surety" for his future good behavior might be imprisoned for a term not exceeding seven years. There were, of course, many additional misdemeanors for which one might be imprisoned at the discretion of the court.

The Civil War was followed by an increase in crime, and new methods of dealing with the offender throughout the South. In this crime wave there were added to the crimes by white people, which were the natural aftermath of war, the offenses of the newly liberated Negroes confused by the responsibilities of freedom, misled sometimes by unwise political advisers, receiving too often hostility and injustice from their white neighbors, and frequently the tools of white criminals craftier than they. "Crime increased and morals degenerated" says Hamilton writing of conditions in North Carolina. "Theft became so common that it was a ·menace to prosperity. Live stock was stolen until in some communities the raising of sheep and hogs was abandoned. Farm products of all sorts were taken to such an extent that the profits of a farm were often thereby swept away. This was partly due to the natural propensities of the Negroes, intensified by their necessities, but they were also encouraged in it by white thieves who dealt largely in farm products purchased at night in small quantities with no questions asked. This evil assumed such proportions that the legislature of 1871 passed a law forbidding the purchase of such commodities after dark."[1]

The number of offenders to be punished by imprisonment in North Carolina was further greatly increased by the change in the methods of punishment under the constitution of 1868. This constitution declared that the only forms of punishment in the state should be death, imprisonment with or without hard labor, and fine. It also further limited the number of crimes for which the legislature might prescribe the death penalty to four. The first legislature under the constitution chose to prescribe the death penalty for only two crimes— murder and rape. Arson was made punishable by life imprisonment.[2] The crimes for which the punishment had been mutilation, whipping, or the

---

[1] J. G. de R. Hamilton, *History of North Carolina*, volume III, "North Carolina After 1860," Chicago, The Lewis Publishing Company, 1919, p. 163.
[2] *N. C. Public Laws*, 1868-69, chapter 167.

pillory under the harsher laws of the period that was ending had to be dealt with in some other way, and imprisonment easily became the method in most cases. All other crimes formerly punished by death were to be punished by imprisonment for six months to ten years, and by fines ranging from one hundred dollars to ten thousand dollars. The reformers of the day, too, who had visions of a penitentiary where men would be reclaimed and retrained for useful citizenship, advocated longer terms of imprisonment. [3]

It was under these conditions that a new prison system—new at least for that section—had its beginnings in the South. The system was usually two-fold. There was a state prison, or state control of certain prisoners, and there was at the same time county control of certain prisoners, usually those with short sentences. For the first class most of the states developed the lease system under which the prisoners were sold to corporations for a period. In some of the states the counties too followed the lead of the central government and leased their prisoners. Florida has only recently given up this method of disposing of county prisoners. In a number of the states there gradually came into existence what has come to be known as the county chain gang system, under which the prisoners under county control are used in the building and repair of the public roads.

For a number of years the great majority of prisoners in both state and county prison systems were Negroes. At the present time, especially in

---

[3] First *Report*, N. C. State Board of Charities, 1870, p. 8.

the county chain gangs, the Negroes still furnish a quota greatly out of proportion to the part which they form of the population. Some figures for the State Prison of North Carolina will give an idea of the proportion of Negro to white prisoners. Accurate figures for county chain gangs of the earlier period are not available. In 1874, of 455 prisoners in the state prison, 384 were Negroes and 71 white. Of the 214 received that year, 190 were Negroes and 24 white. In 1875, of 647 prisoners, 569 were Negroes and 78 white. That year 440 prisoners were received, of whom 395 were Negroes and 45 were white. In 1878, there were 952 prisoners under the control of the state prison board. Of this number, 846 were Negroes, 105 were white, and one was an Indian. [4] These are the proportions that were found in a state where the Negroes form somewhat less than one-third of the population. Similar proportions are found in other Southern states. Aside from the question concerning the justice of the courts in dealing with the Negro offender, the early development of the prison system in the South cannot be understood without reference to the fact that within the two decades following the Civil War the problem of the Southern prison, state and county, became preëminently the problem of dealing with the Negro prisoner. It was this race that furnished the bulk of the prisoners that were employed in the development of the county chain gang, and that still furnishes the large majority of the prisoners used in these gangs.

---

[4] Biennial reports of the North Carolina State Prison, 1874-1878.

As has already been said, most of the Southern states developed some sort of county prison labor system, and in a number of them these prisoners came to be worked on the roads. It should be borne in mind, however, that in the early days of its history the county chain gang marked a stage in the development of penal methods common to the whole country. That legal sanctions for county chain gangs at one time existed in many sections of the United States is shown in a study of convict labor by the Federal Commissioner of Labor published in 1886. [5] The survey showed that most of the Southern states had already developed, so far at least as legislation was concerned, the system of working prisoners on the public roads which has come to be known as the county chain gang system. The states which had made provision for such use of county convict labor on the public roads were Alabama, Arkansas, Florida, Georgia, Mississippi, North Carolina, Tennessee, and Texas. In Alabama, Florida, Georgia, Mississippi, and Tennessee the county authorities might hire or lease such prisoners instead of working them on the roads. In some of the states they might also be worked on a county farm. In Texas the prisoner might avoid labor by the payment of one dollar a day. The Alabama law specifically provided that such prisoners should be chained or otherwise shackled and guarded while at work.

Outside the South eighteen states and territories provided by law for the working of prisoners sentenced to jail on streets or public roads. These

[5] U. S. Commissioner of Labor, *Second Annual Report: Convict Labor*, 1886, pp. 508 ff.

states were California, Colorado, Dakota, Delaware, Illinois, Indiana, Iowa, Kansas, Michigan, Missouri, Montana, Nebraska, Nevada, New Jersey, New Mexico, New York, Utah, and Washington. Kentucky and Maryland provided for the hiring out of such prisoners. The Colorado law provided that county prisoners worked on the public roads should be "well and securely chained and secured." In Dakota the sheriff under whose supervison such prisoners were to be worked was charged to "take all necessary precaution to prevent said convict's escape by ball and chain or otherwise." In Illinois the official in charge of county prisoners must "provide for the safekeeping of such persons . . . by providing balls and chains, and attaching them to such person at any time." In Kansas "the board of county commissioners of any county . . . may, whenever they deem it advisable to do so, properly shackle and work" male prisoners sentenced to jail. In Michigan, when jail prisoners were worked in the streets or highways, they must be "well chained and secured." In Montana in the case of prisoners sentenced to jail, "the sheriff may procure chains for the safekeeping of such prisoner or prisoners and hire out or put to labor such prisoner or prisoners." In New Mexico prisoners used in cleaning streets might be secured by ball and chain. In New York, county prisoners employed on public avenues, highways, and streets must be "well chained and secured." In Washington, prisoners worked on the streets, etc., must "wear an ordinary ball and chain, while performing such labor."

Partly because climatic conditions in the Northern states were not so favorable to outdoor work;

partly, perhaps, because of the influence of the earlier development of manufacturing industries in that section; and partly, no doubt, due to an earlier development of a sensitiveness on the part of the public to the degrading spectacle of men worked in public in chains, it came to be the policy throughout the North and West to work the more desperate and less reliable prisoners within the walls of the prison, and when prisoners were used on road work to employ only honor men.

In the South, on the other hand, the chain gang system has persisted. There is little doubt that the development of this plan of using county prisoners in the construction and maintenance of roads in the South has been influenced, as has already been suggested, by the presence of the Negro. There is still less reason to doubt that the presence of this race has been a factor in the continuance of the system. The mild southern climate, also, has played an important part in the establishment of the county chain gang, because in the South it is practical to work prisoners in the open at all seasons at a minimum cost for clothing and housing.

In North Carolina, as in other Southern states, the county chain gang developed in the first quarter of the century following the Civil War. Except a law on the statute books of the state from 1787 to 1797 authorizing sheriffs to hire out any person who was unable or unwilling to pay costs assessed against him by the court, the only instances of legal provision for labor in connection with offenses against the law in this state prior to the Civil War occur in connection with free Negroes. The first of these is an act of 1787 prohibiting free Negroes and mulattoes entertaining any slave on the Sabbath or at night and providing that if any such free Negro were unable to pay the fine of twenty shillings for the first offense or forty shillings for any subsequent offense he should be sold at auction, after being advertised ten days, for the shortest time for which any one would pay the fine and costs. [6] This act as well as the one applicable to insolvent prisoners in general, it seems, was repealed by the legislature of 1797, but a case involving a free Negro reached the Supreme Court in 1828. [7]

In 1831, the legislature enacted a law providing "that when any free Negro or free person of colour, shall be hereafter convicted of an offense against the criminal laws of the State, and sentenced to pay a fine, and it shall appear to the satisfaction of the court that the free Negro or free person of colour so convicted is unable to pay the fine imposed, the court shall direct the sheriff of the county where such fine is imposed, to hire out the free Negro or free person of colour so convicted to any person who will pay the fine for his services for the shortest space of time." The sheriff must hire such person publicly at the courthouse door. The person hiring such free Negro must give bond for his proper treatment similar to an apprenticeship bond, and has the same authority over the person so hired as the master over his apprentice. In case no one would pay the fine, then the person should

---

[6] *Martin's Revisal*, chapter 6, section II, p. 432.
[7] *N. C. Supreme Court Reports*, 12: 507, *State vs. N. Hood.*

be hired to whoever would pay the most for five years' service. [8]

In 1837, in a case [9] in which the question of the constitutionality of the law was raised, the Supreme Court found that since it could dispose of the case in the interest of the defendant without deciding this question, it would ''be indecent and improper to pronounce any opinion upon so weighty a matter as the constitutionality of an act of the legislature.'' This law discriminating against persons who happened to have Negro blood although they were "free" continued in force until the Civil War. Additional light on the attitude of the public toward these people is shown in a case before the Supreme Court in 1860 [10] in which a free Negro, Richard Fisher, convicted of a misdemeanor, was hired to one Peacock. In an attempt to make him give evidence against himself in another case, Norman, presumably an officer, with the approval of Peacock, whipped Fisher. Norman was indicted and was found not guilty. The State appealed. The Supreme Court decided that the master to whom such a prisoner had been hired might whip for correction but not for an unlawful purpose, such as forcing evidence against one's self. "The five blows inflicted," concludes Judge Manly who wrote the opinion for the court, "under the circumstances, make it a case of minor importance; but, nevertheless, we think . . . that it is technically an indictable battery."

---

[8] *N. C. Laws*, 1831, chapter 13.
[9] *N. C. Supreme Court Reports*, 19: 435, *State vs. Chas. Oxendine.*
[10] *Ibid.*, 53: 220, *State vs. N. Norman.*

The legislature of 1866-67 authorized the justices of the county courts (composed of the justices of the peace) and the judges of the superior courts in all cases where the punishment already prescribed by law did not extend to the loss of life, to sentence the offender to work in chain gangs on the public roads of the county or on any railroad or other work of internal improvement in the state for "such length of time as the court in the exercise of its discretion may see fit, not to exceed one year." In case such prisoners should be worked on the public roads, the county court should employ overseers who should have charge of the prisoners, but when they were hired to a railroad or other corporation, the corporation must furnish guards. If a prisoner should escape, he must serve double the unexpired term. [11]

The legislature of 1872-73 enacted a very similar law. The county commissioners of the various counties were authorized to work on the public roads and streets or to hire out to any county, corporation, or individual engaged on any work of a public nature, prisoners sentenced to the county jail. Such prisoners might not be taken from the county without the consent of the county commissioners given in writing. The commissioners must provide in the contract for the "proper and safekeeping of said convicts." This act was to apply to felons and other offenders for whom the punishment "may be hard labor or imprisonment for one year." [12]

Chapter 113, Public Laws of 1874-75, extends this law to include any person convicted of any

[11] *N. C. Public Laws*, 1866-67, chapter 30.
[12] *N. C. Public Laws*, 1872-73, chapter 174, section 10.

criminal offense in any court, and to those liable for costs.

The constitution of 1868 provided that the only punishment for crime in North Carolina should be death, imprisonment with or without hard labor, and fines. In 1875 this section was modified to provide that this section should be "construed to authorize the employment of such convict labor on public work, or highways, or other labor for public benefit and the farming out thereof, where and in such manner as may be provided by law." This section of the constitution further provides that no prisoner whose labor may be farmed out shall be punished for failure of duty as a laborer except by a responsible officer of the state and that prisoners farmed out shall be at all times, as to their government and discipline, under the supervision and control of the penitentiary board or some officer of the state. [13]

The general assembly of 1876-77 provided that the county commissioners of any county or such other county authorities as might be established by law, and mayors of cities or towns should have power to provide, under such rules and regulations as they may deem best, for the employment on the public streets, public highways, public works, or

---

[13] *Constitution of North Carolina*, article XI, section 1.

The failure of the county chain gang to develop in the years immediately following the earlier legislation on the subject was due perhaps, at least in part, t͞ an order of General Sickles, Military Governor, forbidding corporal punishment as a legal penalty for offenses against the law and the construction of this order to prohibit the use of ball and chain on prisoners.—Governor Jonathan Worth, *Executive Correspondence*, Vol. 1, p. 542; J. G. de R. Hamilton, *Reconstruction in North Carolina*, N. Y., Columbia University, 1914, p. 224.

other labor for individuals or corporations, of all persons imprisoned in the county jails as punishment for violation of the laws or for non-payment of fine and costs. Such prisoners were not to be detained beyond the time fixed by the courts, and were to be under the supervision of the sheriff of the county in which such prisoner was convicted, or his deputy; "and the sheriff, or his deputy, shall be deemed a state officer for the purpose of this act." . . . "The party in whose service said convicts may be, may use the necessary means to hold and keep them in custody and to prevent their escape." The punishment for escape was fixed at thirty days imprisonment or fifty dollars fine. [14]

In 1878, in the case of *State vs. Shaft*, [15] a case in which a man was hired out to his wife, Justice Rodman, in handing down the opinion of the court, suggested that the legislature might see fit to amend the law so as to leave it to the judge to say whether a prisoner may be hired out or not. The next year, 1879, the legislature added to the law the proviso: "It shall not be lawful to farm out any such convicted person who may be imprisoned for the non-payment of a fine, or as a punishment imposed for the offense of which he may have been convicted, unless the court before whom the trial is had shall in its judgment so authorize." [16] This provision in the opinion of the Supreme Court applies only to the hiring to individuals and corporations. [17]

[14] *N. C. Public Laws*, 1876-77, chapter 196.
[15] Cited in *N. C. Supreme Court Reports*, 94:807, *State vs. Sneed.*
[16] *N. C. Public Laws*, 1879, chapter 218.
[17] *N. C. Supreme Court Reports*, 94: 807, *State vs. Sneed.*

These laws brought down to date give us sections 1356 and 1358 of the Consolidated Statutes of 1919, which read:

1356. *Counties and towns may hire out certain prisoners.* The board of commissioners of the several counties, within their respective jurisdictions, or such other county authorities therein as may be established, and the mayor and intendant of the several cities and towns of the state, have power to provide under such rules and regulations as they may deem best for the employment on the public streets, public highways, public works, or other labor for individuals or corporations, of all persons imprisoned in the jails of their respective counties, cities and towns, upon conviction of any crime or misdemeanor, or who may be committed to jail for failure to enter into bond for keeping the peace or for good behavior, and who fail to pay all the costs which they are adjudged to pay, or to give good and sufficient security therefor: Provided, such prisoner or convict shall not be detained beyond the time fixed by the judgment of the court. The amount realized from hiring out such persons shall be credited to them for the fine and bill of costs in all cases of conviction. It is unlawful to farm out any such convicted person who may be imprisoned for the nonpayment of a fine, or as punishment imposed for the offense of which he may have been convicted, unless the court before whom the trial is had shall in its judgment so authorize.

1358. *Sheriff to have control of prisoners hired out.* All convicts hired or farmed out by the county or other municipal authorities shall at all times be under the supervision and control, as to their government and discipline, of the sheriff, or his deputy, of the county in which they were convicted and imprisoned and the sheriff, or his deputy, shall be deemed a state officer for the purpose of this section.

This law has been used, apparently, mainly as a basis for the custom of allowing the county com-

missioners to hire out certain prisoners to individuals. The caption for 1356 in the Consolidated
Statutes reads: "Counties and towns may hire
out certain prisoners." It has often been used
beneficently in the interest of youthful prisoners,
in cases where some good man has been willing to
take such offender under his care and guidance for
a period. It has also been used for the exploitation
of the labor of prisoners, especially Negro prisoners,
by the individuals hiring them, with the knowledge
and consent of county officials, if not of the courts
themselves. The extent of such exploitation awaits
careful study. [18]

These sections of law also lay the legal foundation for a county convict lease system. Since 1879
such a system can develop only with the consent
of the court—the Superior Court, the county recorder's court, or such other inferior court as has

---

[18] Jerome Dowd, in what is at once a defense of this practice
and an apology for it, says: The term peonage as used in the
South has grown out of a court practice which was solely humanitarian in its motive and was designed especially to favor Negro
offenders. When white people are fined for a minor offense they
usually are able to raise the money from some relative or friend
and thus avoid going to jail. In order to give the Negro an equal
opportunity to escape a jail sentence, laws were made which
provided that persons unable to pay a fine might be bound out or
bailed to any one who would pay the fine. Under these laws
Negro offenders have been bailed to any man who needed their
labor, and have been deprived of their freedom until the fine was
worked out. Although the kind of Negroes who have to be bailed
are not the best workers, and while the white people who do bailing are not the best type of farmers, perhaps nine-tenths of the
cases of bailing are terminated according to agreement and without injustice to the bailee. In a great many cases the white man
who pays the fine is a friend of the Negro and allows him his freedom and trusts him to repay the amount of the fine when convenient or at a specified date. Where abuses have arisen from
this bailing process they have been neither designed nor foreseen.
The Negro in American Life, New York, The Century Co.,
1926, p. 132.

the right to sentence offenders to jail. One such case has recently developed in the state. In 1923, eight men—six white men and two Negroes—were sentenced by the Superior Court of Watauga County to jail to be assigned by the county commissioners to the roads of any county with which they could make the necessary arrangements. (Watauga does not maintain a road gang.) It happened that none of the counties to which this county is accustomed to send prisoners wanted prisoners at this particular time. The chairman of the board of county commissioners, thereupon, went to see the judge before whom the men had been tried and secured his consent to hire the men to a contractor doing road work. The consent of the judge given after court had adjourned for the session was, it seems, without sanction of law and no record was made of it on the minutes of the court. Nevertheless, the men were hired to a contractor in Iredell County. At the suggestion of the attorney for the contractor the sheriff of Watauga County appointed two employees of the contracting company in Iredell County who were unknown to him as his deputies. The Attorney-General is of the opinion that this appointment of deputies was legal under section 1358 of the Consolidated Statutes given above. The only thing illegal about this transaction, therefore, was that the judge gave his consent to a change in sentence after court had adjourned for the session. [19]

[19] *Biennial Report*, N. C. State Board of Charities and Public Welfare, 1922-24, p. 65; Files State Board of Charities and Public Welfare; *Biennial Report*, Attorney-General of N. C., 1922-24, p. 249.

The legislature in 1866 passed a law which provided that the justices of the courts of pleas and quarter sessions might establish houses of correction. Five to nine directors were to be appointed, which directors might be the wardens of the poor. These directors were to make by-laws and regulations, such regulations to be approved by the county court. The justices were to appoint the manager who must be bonded. Any prisoner who should escape might upon being recaptured be put in fetters or shackles or closely confined in the county jail or elsewhere at the discretion of the manager and held for an additional period of thirty days. [20] The next session provided that two or more counties might unite in establishing a house of correction. [21] These institutions are called in the caption to the first act "work-houses."

A law enacted by the legislature of 1870-71, after providing that prisoners who had been sentenced for a term of two years or more to the new penitentiary should be received at once and that those whose sentences were for less than two years, as early as practicable, provided further:

. . . That the county commissioners of any county may provide for the employment of all convicts who have heretofore been sentenced to the penitentiary for a time less than two years, now remaining in the jails, work-houses or prisons, or that may hereafter be sentenced to imprisonment with hard labor for any time less than two years, as prescribed in chapter thirty-five of the public laws of 1866, . . . and all powers given to the justices of the court of pleas and

[20] N. C. *Public Laws*, 1865-66, chapter 35.
[21] N. C. *Public Laws*, 1866-67, chapter 130.

quarters session in said chapter are hereby conferred upon the boards of county commissioners of the several counties of the State and in addition to the mode of employment prescribed in said chapter such convicts may be employed in working upon the public roads or in any other useful labor the commissioners may order, and such guards may be employed as may be necessary to secure such convicts while at labor, and to take them forth and return them to the jail or workhouse when not employed in labor; and all powers given to the managers of the workhouse in said chapter are hereby conferred upon any officer appointed to take charge of such convicts, or upon the sheriffs of the respective counties. The commissioners shall have the same power of providing for the expense of working the public roads by convicts as are given to the justices of the county court for erecting workhouses and employing convicts.[22]

Another act of the same legislature [23] providing for the building of a turnpike from Statesville to Mount Airy, authorized the directors of the road to make requisition on the county commissioners of the counties through which the road was to be built for all convicts sentenced to the penitentiary for a term of two years or less. The directors were to employ "faithful and energetic" overseers whose duty it should be to keep the convicts "industriously employed." "In order to enable said overseers to control and prevent said convicts from making their escape, said overseer" was authorized and empowered "to confine said convicts together with chain, or if need be with ball and chain."

In 1876 a similar law provided that all prisoners sentenced to the jails of Burke, McDowell, Mitch-

[22] *N. C. Public Laws*, 1870-71, chapter 124.
[23] *Ibid.*, chapter 251.

ell, and Yancey counties for less than one year should be available upon demand of the commissioners in charge for work on the Buck Creek, the Jonas Ridge, and the John's River turnpikes. [24]

An act of 1879 assigned all prisoners sentenced to jail for less than one year in Stokes County to work in building a public road in that county. All those imprisoned for non-payment of costs were likewise to work at a price per month to be fixed by the court. [25] Another act of the same year [26] authorized the commissioners of Craven County to make requisition upon the sheriff for all prisoners sentenced to the penitentiary for one year and to work these and all other prisoners sentenced to jail in that county upon the public works of the county.

The legislature at the special session of 1880 enacted a road law, later known as the Mecklenburg Road Law, that provided among other things for the working of prisoners on the roads. The law was limited in its application to Mecklenburg, Forsyth, and Stokes counties. Prisoners sentenced to jail as a punishment or for non-payment of fines and those sentenced to the penitentiary who were not required to be kept in the penitentiary were to be available to the county commissioners for road work. The commissioners were empowered to farm out such prisoners to any person or persons for work on the highways and to furnish such persons the "necessary shackles, implements, and tools" for such work. Those working out fines or costs should be credited with such amount per day

[24] N. C. Public Laws, 1876-77 chapter 20.
[25] N. C. Public Laws, 1879, chapter 39.
[26] Ibid., chapter 270.

as the road supervisors thought they were worth. [27]
Another act of the same session gave Lenoir County
practically the same authority as to working
prisoners. [28]

In the Code of 1883 among the duties of county
commissioners enumerated is the following:

To provide for the employmen˙ on the highway or
public works of the county, of all persons condemned
to imprisonment with hard labor, and not sent to the
penitentiary. [29]

The Mecklenburg law, which was repealed in
1881, was reënacted with modifications in 1885 for
Mecklenburg County only. [30] Finally in 1887 [31] and
1889 [32] there was enacted the legislation which
governs the county road gangs at the present time.
This law forms sections 1359, 1360, and 1361 of the
Consolidated Statutes of 1919 and is as follows:

1359. *Convicts who may be sentenced to or worked on
roads.* When any county has made provision for the
working of convicts upon the public roads, or when any
number of counties have jointly made provision for
working convicts upon the public roads, it is lawful for
and the duty of the judge holding court in such counties
to sentence to imprisonment at hard labor on the public
roads for such terms as are now prescribed by law for
their imprisonment in the county jail or in the State's
Prison, the following classes of convicts: First, all persons convicted of offenses the punishment whereof
would otherwise be wholly, or in part, imprisonment

[27] *N. C. Public Laws*, 1880, extra session, chapter 19.
[28] *Ibid.*, chapter 50.
[29] *N. C. Code*, 1883, section 707, subsection 18.
[30] *N. C. Public Laws*, 1885, chapter 134.
[31] *N. C. Public Laws*, 1887, chapter 355.
[32] *N. C. Public Laws*, 1889, chapter 419.

in the common jail; second, all persons convicted of crimes the punishment whereof would otherwise, wholly or in part, be imprisonment in the State's Prison for a term not exceeding ten years.

In such counties there may be worked on the public roads, in like manner, all persons sentenced to imprisonment in jail by any magistrate; and also, all insolvents imprisoned by any court in said counties for non-payment of costs in criminal causes may be retained in imprisonment and worked on the public roads until they repay the county to the extent of the half fees charged up against the county for each person taking the insolvent oath. The rate of compensation to be allowed each insolvent for work on the public roads shall be fixed by the county commissioners at a just and fair compensation, regard being had to the amount of work of which each insolvent is capable.

1360. *Deductions from sentence allowed for good behavior.* When a convict has been sentenced to work upon the public roads of a county, and has faithfully performed the duties assigned to him during his term of sentence, he is entitled to a deduction from the time of his sentence of five days for each month, and he shall be discharged from the county roads when he has served his sentence, less the number of days he may be entitled to have deducted. The authorities having him in charge shall be the sole judges as to the faithful performance of the duties assigned to him. Should he escape or attempt to escape he shall forfeit and lose any deduction he may have been entitled to prior to that time. This section shall apply also to women sentenced to a county farm or county home.

1361. *Convicts sentenced to roads to be under county control.* The convicts sentenced to hard labor upon the public roads, under second section preceding, shall be under the control of the county authorities, and the county authorities have power to enact all needful rules and regulations for the successful working of convicts on the public roads or in canaling the main drains and swamps or on other public work of the county.

To this has been added Section 4409 of the Consolidated Statutes:

If any officer, either judical, executive or ministerial, shall order or require the working of any female on the streets or roads in any group or chain gang in the State, he shall be deemed guilty of a misdemeanor.

In theory, therefore, the county chain gang has developed from the "house of correction" as provided for in the constitution, which came to be known as the county "workhouse" in actual practice. The law of 1866-67, as has been pointed out, gave authority for working prisoners on the roads as well as for hiring them out; but the emphasis here, in the law makers' minds has always been on the hiring out. The 1870-71 act, on the other hand, is specifically connected by the language of the law itself with the "workhouse" law of 1866, and the two acts are brought down to date in two sections of the Consolidated Statutes, the one announcing by its caption that it is a law designed primarily to permit the hiring out of prisoners and the other furnishing the legal basis for the county chain gang. We shall see presently that in actual practice also the chain gang grew out of the workhouse.

The first road, or in this case street working, gang in the state, perhaps, was organized under the military government immediately following the Civil War. In the Raleigh *Daily Standard* for September 27, 1865, appears this item:

The military on yesterday picked up a large number of gentlemen of color, who were loitering about the street corners, apparently much depressed by ennui and general lassitude of the nervous system, and, having armed them with spades and shovels, set them to play at street cleaning for the benefit of their own health and the health of the town generally. This is certainly a "move in the right direction;" for the indolent, lazy, Sambo, who lies about in the sunshine and neglects to seek employment by which to make a living, is undoubtedly "the right man in the right place" when enrolled in the spade and shovel brigade.

In the period of almost twenty years between the enactment of the first law in 1866 permitting the use of the labor of certain prisoners on the public roads of the counties and the passage of the Mecklenburg Road Law in 1885, there were occasional instances of the use of prisoners on road and street work, but no established policy of using convict labor as a means to develop and maintain a system of roads. [33] One finds occasional references to work by prisoners in the newspapers of the period referred to. In the Raleigh *Daily Sentinel* of June 27, 1871, for instance, appears this item in the report of the mayor's court:

Providence Buncombe, Colored, arrested by officer Webb, charged with creating a disturbance on the premises of Mr. W. W. West; put on street gang.

In the same newspaper in the issue of August 28, 1872, appears this item of news from Weldon:

The jail birds, engineered by some of the Halifaxians, have greatly improved the streets and sidewalks, and old Halifax looks as if a new leaf had been suddenly turned over.

[33] J. A. Holmes, *Improvement of Public Roads in North Carolina*, 1895, Washington, Government Printing Office, p. 514.

After the reënactment of the Mecklenburg Road Law in 1885 and especially after the passage of the general law in 1887 the chain gang system developed rather rapidly in the state. The story of the beginning in Mecklenburg, as told in a bulletin of the United States Department of Agriculture, from information furnished by Mr. McDonald, a member of the county road commission, is that interest in the possibility of using the prisoners confined in the county jail to build roads arose after a man who had leased a group of prisoners from the county had employed them successfully in building a cotton mill. At first only Charlotte Township was willing to levy the special tax necessary to organize the work. This township "organized the thirty convicts into a roadbuilding squad, by placing over them a competent superintendent and two guards." At first the stone used in building macadam roads was broken by hand by the prisoners. As the work progressed the other townships of the county "fell into line," machinery was purchased, the convict force increased, and the work in every way organized on a larger scale. [34]

It has already been suggested that the chain gang is a development or modification of the workhouse; so it will not be surprising to find that in the early days the prisoners working on the roads were quartered in the workhouse which, following ancient custom, was built in connection with the poorhouse or in close proximity to it. Prisoners, in 1887, probably from the workhouse were employed

---

[34] U. S. Department of Agriculture, Office of Road Inquiry, *Bulletin*, number 16 (Revised), 1898, p. 20.

on the roads of Wake County. [35] In the report of the State Board of Charities for 1889-90 appears this entry in regard to Wake County:

"The poor house and workhouse are within the same enclosure, but separated by broken ground. Prisoners sixty; guarded and worked on county roads." [36] Four years later (1893) the Secretary of the Board in his report says in discussing the herding of prisoners together without classification:

Another branch of this evil is the practice of sentencing men to the county workhouse for infraction of city ordinances where a slight misdemeanor which may be atoned for by a trival fine and cost, must in the case of a man too poor to pay even an insignificant sum, be punished by hard labor on the county roads, in company with felons—often degraded convicts—under sentences for loathsome or desperate crimes. These anomalies call loudly for correction, and ought to reach the ears and consciences of our lawmakers. [37]

In 1894, the Secretary writes at greater length of this "newly-organized" county workhouse:

The men of experience in connection with penal institutions in North Carolina feel that the weakest point in our system for the repression of crime is the newly-organized county workhouse, and it becomes this board to speak a word of warning. Actuated by a desire to relieve the taxpayer of the burden of maintenance in the penitentiary—so heavy and grievous in our State for many years, and ardently seeking means to improve our county roads, as one of the greatest needs of the present day—institutions have grown up in vari-

---

[35] *N. C. Supreme Court Reports*, 98: 685, *State vs. Weathers.*
[36] *Biennial Report*, N. C. State Board of Charities 1889-90, p. 11.
[37] *Biennial Report*, N. C. State Board of Charities, 1893-95, p. 16.

ous counties under the recent statutes, which may be termed "little penitentiaries." Unfortunately, they must, for the most part, be managed by officers without penal experience, and they are, as yet, largely without proper means for the control with discretion and efficiency.

Errors in management have crept in, in both directions. In a few cases we hear of a laxity of control beyond belief. Men, convicted of felonious offenses, who would have formerly spent years within the State prison, are organized loosely into a road-working force, with so little discipline that cases are reported of their being allowed to spend the night at their own homes occasionally, returning on parole to the work. It is proper to say that we have no official report of such a case communicated to this office, but it has been stated by gentlemen of veracity that such habits exist in certain counties; unwarranted, of course, by law, and tending to bring its stern mandates into contempt.

But the danger is chiefly in the other direction, of cruel and inhuman management, on account of the ignorance and inexperience of guards and overseers, or of the misapprehension of the rights of the convict by the authorities of the county. There are shining illustrations to the contrary, as in the effective but just administration of the workhouse in Wake. On the other hand, the county of Mecklenburg, which has so admirably refitted her jail and county home, maintains a system of loading with ball and chain the convict on the roads or in the quarry, in addition to the armed guard, to prevent elopement.

This is torture instead of punishment, and it has been earnestly protested against, in correspondence from this office, as unwarranted by the law, which, it must not be forgotten, sacredly guards the "security, health and comfort" of the prisoner. It is hoped and believed that the new Board of Commissioners of that county will accord a favorable hearing to the protest which, in behalf of this board, has been made by Commissioner S. W. Reid, who has earned the right to special recognition by long and patriotic service to his country. . . . [38]

In the report for 1897-98, in suggesting the practicability of using workhouse prisoners to cultivate the poorfarms and thus contribute to the support of the inmates of the poorhouses, the Secretary notes the growing tendency to work such prisoners on the public roads. [39]

By 1896 the system had grown to such proportions that the warden of the state prison in his report lists it as one of the causes of the decrease in the number of prisoners in his institution.

The increased employment of convicts by counties upon their own roads and farms, at their own expense, works a sensible relief to the State's Prison. It is to be hoped that other counties will follow the example of Mecklenburg, Buncombe, and others, except that they generally send their feeble and disabled men and women to this prison.[40]

In 1902, J. A. Holmes, State Geologist, speaking to the North Carolina Good Roads Convention in Raleigh, stated that in 1901 about twenty-five counties were employing prisoners in road work. Mecklenburg with one hundred had the largest force. The average daily number employed by these counties was 675. In the same convention, Duff Merrick of Buncombe County reported: "We think with the exception of Mecklenburg, we can say we have more macadamized roads than any

[38] *Biennial Report*, N. C. State Board of Charities, 1893-95, pp. 122 and 123.
[39] *Ibid.*, 1897-98, p. 42.
[40] *Report*, N. C. Penitentiary, 1895-96, p. 7.

other county in the State. . . . So far we have built our roads by using the convicts from the county, probably fifty on an average." R. W. Hobgood reported: "Four or five years ago Granville [County] had a workhouse and we had fifteen or twenty convicts. The county commissioners employed an engineer to take those convicts in hand and go to work on the roads. They graded some road and it stands yet." S. H. Webb of Alamance County said: "About thirteen years ago we put our convicts to work on the public roads. Our convict force numbers about thirty." J. Van Lindley of Guilford County reported that about thirteen years ago two townships in which Greensboro is located levied a road tax. Three years later other townships joined them. "Then we worked our convicts on the roads and the convicts from adjoining counties. For a few years we went ahead with a large force of convicts and graded all the leading roads in the county—about one hundred and seventy miles." Paul C. Graham of Durham County said: "We have also the convict system. Every person convicted in Durham, except those sentenced for long terms, is put to work on the public roads. In addition we get convicts from adjoining counties. We have on the roads of Durham convicts from Alamance and Person counties. The law permits this to be done."

W. C. McMacken, superintendent of roads of Wake County, talked at some length:

Our labor is that of convicts. . . . Our convicts cost us at the present prices of provisions seventeen and one-half cents per capita per day to feed, clothe, and guard them, and give them medical attention. I have handled over eleven hundred convicts since I have been in this business and have yet to find one that did not give me all the work required of him. Convicts are very different beings from what a great many people suppose. Most of them are soft-hearted sympathetic fellows, willing to do whatever we require of them, from the fact that we treat them humanely, look after their health, and protect them in every way. Then when I call for work, I get it, and they give it cheerfully and willingly. Give me convicts, six-inch-tired dump wagons, and good mules to build roads.[41]

The county chain gang, as an important factor in road construction developed, as we have seen, within the last fifteen years of the last century, and by the opening of the present century was in use in twenty-five counties including practically all of those that were showing particular interest in the movement for improved roads. This method of punishing offenders as it appeared soon after the close of the period under consideration, with its inevitable limitations and weaknesses, is discussed at some length in the biennial report of Superintendent J. L. Mann of the State Prison, for 1907-08, with a quotation from which we may well conclude this chapter:

Under special acts of the Legislature about forty counties in North Carolina have organized what are known as chain gangs and use them in the construction and improvement of their public roads and highways. From the report of the Board of Public Charities it will be found that there are more than 1,200 prisoners in these chain gangs serving sentence for crime. The State has granted to the counties absolutely and unconditionally the full management and control of these

[41] *Proceedings*, N. C. Good Roads Convention, Raleigh, 1902

prisoners, and has endeavored to surrender its responsibility for them, not even reserving a supervisory or inspectionary authority. Without the least concert with one another, each county is in supreme control of its own gang, prescribes its own rules of discipline, of clothing, of feeding, of guarding, of quartering and of working. Consequently, in addition to what is known as the State's Prison, North Carolina has forty wholly independent State prisons, under forty separate and distinct managements, with forty different and distinct sets of rules and regulations, and over which there is absolutely no State supervision and inspection. The hospital facilities, at least, of all these many prisons are inadequate and defective, for in none of the counties is there a place, except the jail or workhouse quarters, where the sick or the enfeebled or the demented can be cared for and cured. I have been informed, but cannot substantiate the statement, that the average life of a road convict is less than five years. All prisoners are at least human beings, very many are intelligent, and some are possessed of refined sensibilities. A large proportion of them are capable certainly of serving their sentences and afterwards of becoming useful citizens. None are mere working machines which the State could condemn to unremitting toil and unendurable hardships, only to be worn out and buried within a few months, or, at most, in a few years. The law evidently intends the punishment to fit the crime, and that persons convicted of felony and given long terms shall be sent to the State's Prison, while those convicted of less serious offenses, especially misdemeanors, shall be given shorter terms and lighter work upon the roads. And yet, under existing conditions, it is strangely true that harsher and more vigorous punishment is inflicted upon the petty offender than upon him who commits the more serious crime.

The present chain gang policy of our State—it is in no sense a system—cannot be successfully defended, and ought to be at once discontinued. The civilization of our age demands it. I believe it to be in every respect as defective and as full of possibilities for wrongdoing, cruelty and inhumanity as was the old convict-lease system, now long since abolished. I do not mean to charge that acts of cruelty and brutality have been actually committed in any county, nor that the prisoners of any county have suffered from overwork and neglect, but I do mean that the possibility for such things has existed and does exist, and, if the present policy is continued, I feel it will be only a matter of time when it will bring upon our State deserved criticism and an unenviable notoriety. The State cannot surrender nor evade responsibility for those whom it has fettered for crime. . . . [42]

---

[42] *Biennial Report*, North Carolina State Prison, 1907-08, pp. 11-13.

Chapter III

METHODS OF ORGANIZATION

THE legal sanction for the organization and
control of prison labor used on the county
roads is found in chapter twenty-four,
articles two and nine, and chapter seventy, article
four, of the Consolidated Statutes of North Carolina, and in numerous "public-local" laws applicable usually to a single county, occasionally to two
or more counties. The first of these chapters gives
to the county commissioners the power to lay out,
alter, repair, and discontinue highways, [1] and "to
provide for the employment on the highways or
public works in the county of all persons condemned to imprisonment with hard labor, and not
sent to the penitentiary." [2] Another section de-
fining this power more specifically gives to the
county commissioners, "or such other county
authorities . . . as may be established," power to
provide "under such rules and regulations as they
may deem best," for the employment on the public
roads of persons sentenced to the jails. [3] The law
next provides that when any county has made provision for the working of convicts on the public
roads, or when any number of counties have jointly
made provision for such work, judges may sentence
to the roads those who would otherwise be punished
by imprisonment in the common jail, and those

---

[1] *Consolidated Statutes of North Carolina*, 1297, 18.
[2] *Ibid.*, 1297, 31.
[3] *Ibid.*, 1356.

who might be sentenced to the state prison for a term not exceeding ten years. It further provides that those who are unable to pay fines or costs may also be assigned to labor on the roads. [4] Prisoners thus assigned to the roads are "under the control of the county authorities," and "the county authorities have power to enact all needful rules and regulations for the successful working of convicts upon public roads." [5] The prisoner assigned to the roads has a right to a deduction from his sentence of five days a month for good behavior. [6] Finally the county commissioners are empowered to levy a tax to defray the expenses of working prisoners on the roads. [7]

A later law [8] makes possible a somewhat different organization for the working of prisoners on the county roads by providing for the creation of a county road commission which shall relieve the board of county commissioners of those of its duties pertaining to the construction and maintenance of roads. The law directs that when any county has been organized under the provisions of this article, prisoners sentenced to work on the roads of that county "shall be assigned into the custody and control of the county road commission by the board of county commissioners, when said board is so requested by the county road commissioners." "The county road commission is . . . authorized . . . to divide the prisoners into classes or groups according to the character of the prisoner,

---

[4] *Consolidated Statutes of North Carolina*, 1359.
[5] *Ibid.*, 1361.
[6] *Ibid.*, 1360.
[7] *Ibid.*, 1364.
[8] *Ibid.*, 3643 ff.

and to work any or all such prisoners as they deem best without guards and without stripes." [9]

Here, it seems, is ample authority for the organization of the machinery for the construction and maintenance of a system of roads in any county, including the organization and direction of a force of prisoners for work on the roads. But there is no county in the state now maintaining a force of prisoners on its roads for which there has not been considerable special legislation. The "public-local laws" usually reënact in substance the provisions of chapter twenty-four, article nine, sections 1356 and following, summarized above. These laws often go more into detail as to the employment of a superintendent, guards, and other employees to direct the work of the prisoners and to guard against their escape. If a road commission is formed the law provides for its selection and not infrequently names the first members to constitute such a commission. Sometimes the chief reason for the enactment of such a special law, apparently, is the personnel of the commission. Such a law frequently provides also for the method of selecting a superintendent of roads. It may even name him, although there is already a road commission in existence. [10]

There are four general plans of organization under this multiplicity of laws. Under the first of these plans the county commissioners are charged with the general supervision and control of the prisoners worked on the public roads. Durham County will serve as a type of this method of

---

[9] *Consolidated Statutes of North Carolina,* 3678.
[10] *N. C. Public-Local Laws,* 1923, chapter 434.

organization. The board of county commissioners has general supervision and control of the building and maintenance of the roads of the county. This board elects annually and fixes the salary of a superintendent of roads to whom is assigned the duty of supervising, directing, and having charge of the maintenance and building of all public roads in the county. The board of county commissioners or the road superintendent, subject to the approval of the commissioners, appoints, with power to remove at any time, such guards and other employees as may be needed in connection with the convict force. According to the provisions of the law:

All prisoners confined in the county jail under a final sentence of the court for crime, or imprisonment for non-payment of costs or fines, or under final judgment in cases of bastardy, or under the vagrancy acts, all insolvents who shall be imprisoned by any court in said county for non-payment of costs, and all persons who would otherwise be sentenced in said county to the State's Prison for a term of less than ten years shall be worked on the public roads of the county: *Provided*, that in case of serious physical disability, certified to by the county physician, persons convicted in said superior, criminal, or inferior courts in the county may be sentenced to the penitentiary or to the county jail.

The act provides further that upon application of the commissioners of Durham County judges may sentence prisoners from other counties to work on the roads of that county. [11]

The second type provides for organization under a county road commission. Such a commission may be selected by the board of county commis-

[11] *N. C. Public-Local Laws*, 1913, chapter 463.

sioners, or appointed by the legislature, or elected by a vote of the people, or nominated by the chairmen of the county executive committees of the two major political parties and appointed by the governor. The powers and duties of the county road commission as prescribed in these special laws do not differ materially, especially as they relate to the control and direction of prison labor, from those prescribed for county commissioners. The commission is usually instructed to employ a superintendent of roads and it is empowered to employ such guards and others as are needed. Forsyth County may serve as an example of this type. The local law provides for a commission of three members appointed by the general assembly, one every two years, for a term of six years. Two members are to be selected from the majority political party in the county and one from the minority party. This commission has general control of the building and maintenance of the county roads. They may appoint an engineer, a superintendent of road construction, a superintendent of the convict force, and such other officers or employees as may be necessary. The prisoners in the county chain gang are under their control, and they are specially authorized to classify such prisoners in three grades according to the character and conduct of the prisoner.

In addition to this commission of three, there are elected by the voters of the county, biennially, one road supervisor from each township. These supervisors advise the commission as to road matters in their respective townships, and have charge of such repair work as cannot be done by the "convict force, outfit, and machinery."[12]

Under each of the foregoing plans the county has been organized as a unit. Under a third plan the township is the unit. Hertford County has been operating three chain gangs under this plan, though it has recently discontinued them. The law under which this county has been carrying on its road work provides for a board of road supervisors of three members in each township. These boards are appointed by the county commissioners. "The supervisors of any township in Hertford County, or two or more townships conjointly, through the board of county commissioners of Hertford County may arrange to work county or state convicts on the public roads, and are hereby empowered to use the road fund of the township or townships in so arranging for the working of convicts, to buy the necessary equipment, to properly care for such convicts, and to hire the necessary guards to look after them."[13]

The fourth plan provides for the organization of a special road district. The Rocky Mount Road District is a case in point. This district is composed of several townships in Nash and Edgecombe counties, centering about the city of Rocky Mount. The building and repair of the roads in this district are directed by a commission of five, one appointed by the county commissioners of Nash County, one by the county commissioners of Edgecombe County, and three by the governing body of the

---

[12] N. C. Public-Local Laws, 1913, chapter 12; 1924, extra session, chapter 67.
[13] N. C. Public-Local Laws, 1913, chapter 562.

city of Rocky Mount.   The commission appoints
a superintendent, guards, and other employees
necessary for the operation of the chain gang. [14]

There are several interesting variations from
these types. Cumberland County in 1913 secured
the enactment of a law that provided among other
things that the "board of commissioners may in
their discretion hire out or lease the convicts that
are now or may hereafter be mentioned to work on
the roads of Cumberland County, or any part of
them, to persons, firms, or corporations, in or outside of Cumberland County." [15] Ten years later
Harnett County secured the passage of an almost
identical law permitting the establishment of a
county convict lease system. "If at any time said
prisoners cannot, in the judgment of the highway
commission, be advantageously employed on such
work it shall be lawful for the highway commission
to hire out said prisoners, for reasonable and proper
consideration, as one body, or in a gang or gangs,
to any person, firm or corporation, public or private, for the performance of other kinds of work,
whether road work or other work." [16] Rockingham
County, in 1919, secured the enactment of a special
law providing for the hiring out of the prisoners on
the chain gang at the discretion of the county commissioners, though this law is not so definite in its
language. [17] No one of these counties has yet decided that it is not profitable to work the prisoners
on the roads. No one of them, therefore, has taken
advantage of the authority to lease its prisoners.

[14] *N. C. Public- Laws*, 1907, chapter 814.
[15] *N. C. Public-Local Laws*, 1913, chapter 453.
[16] *N. C. Public-Local Laws*, 1923, chapter 586, section 10.
[17] *N. C. Public-Local Laws*, 1919, chapter 452.

Buncombe County's law provides that only prisoners sentenced for five years or under may be sent to the roads, and, further, that the board of county commissioners may "in its discretion abolish the use of striped prison clothing as a garb for the use of prisoners or convicts in said county of Buncombe altogether." The same law, on the other hand, specifically provides for flogging as a means of discipline, though it attempts to guard against what it terms "cruel and unmerciful" beating. [18]

Chatham County limits her prison road force to misdemeanants. The county commissioners may establish a "convict force or chain gang, to which convict force or chain gang may be sentenced persons convicted of all offenses of the grade of a misdemeanor in the Superior Court of Chatham County, and by mayors or justices of the peace of Chatham County wherein they have final jurisdiction." [19]

Moore County has been enabled to modify the usual plan of organization by working only honor prisoners. A special act for this county provides "that the Moore County Highway Commission is hereby authorized and vested with power to establish reasonable rules and regulations for working convicts upon the public roads of Moore County and that the said commission may direct its superintendent of roads or foreman of road force or forces to establish an honor system and to make trusties of such convicts as may in his or their opinion prove

---

[18] *N. C. Public-Local Laws,* 1923, chapter 328.
[19] *N. C. Public-Local Laws,* 1921, chapter 248.

themselves worthy."[20]   Mr. Leonard Tufts, a former member of the county road commission, says that the county finds it practicable to assign to this honor camp, where they are worked without guards, eighty-five per cent of the prisoners sentenced to the roads in the county. The other fifteen per cent are sent by special arrangement to the chain gang of another county.

Mecklenburg and Wake counties have provided by special law for the assignment of prisoners to their road forces with sentences ranging as high as twenty years.[21]

Rowan County has thought it necessary to give special protection to its officers and citizens in regard to any injury inflicted upon a prisoner.

No superintendent, guard, or other employee of said commissioners shall be held either criminally or civilly liable for any injury inflicted upon any convict in his custody or under his supervision while in good faith or with due care enforcing such discipline as may be necessary to carry out such rules and regulations in the working of convicts upon the highways or public roads as said commissioners may from time to time enact and promulgate. If any superintendent, guard, or other employee who may have such persons in charge shall willfully or negligently permit any prisoner to escape from his custody, such superintendent, guard, or employee, shall be guilty of a misdemeanor, and upon conviction shall be fined or imprisoned in the discretion of the court: *Provided*, that no superintendent, guard or other employee shall be held criminally or civilly liable for inflicting any wound or other injury upon any prisoner who may attempt to escape from his custody or control if such superintendent, guard, or other employee shall

---

[20] *N. C. Public-Local Laws*, 1924, extra session, chapter 162.
[21] *N. C. Public-Local Laws*, 1915, chapter 792.

have reasonable ground to believe it necessary to so wound or otherwise injure such prisoner in order to prevent his actual escape from custody; and any superintendent, guard, or other employee from whose custody any convict shall have escaped, or any other officer or private citizen, shall have the right at any time thereafter to arrest such escaped convict, and to use such means as shall actually be necessary to that end; and no person, in arresting or attempting to arrest any escaped convict, shall be held civilly or criminally liable for any wound or other injury which he may inflict upon such convict while attempting to arrest him, if he shall have reasonable grounds to believe that it was necessary to resort to such means in order to make such arrest.[22]

One city, Greensboro, maintains a gang of its own, to which prisoners are sentenced from the city court.

The typical organization for the working of prisoners on the county roads is composed of the board of county commissioners or a county road commission with general control and direction of the county road system; a superintendent who has general supervision of the prisoners and who usually has numerous other duties in connection with the construction and maintenance of roads; an official usually called a supervisor for each camp or gang of prisoners, who is the foreman in charge of the work of his particular gang and is responsible for the camp and the prisoners under his charge; a guard for every ten to fifteen prisoners worked under the gun, that is, a minimum of two armed guards to the usual squad of twenty to thirty men; one guard for night duty; and usually a steward or

---

[22] *N. C. Public-Local Laws*, 1913, chapter 473, section 6.

yard man who looks after the camp. Occasionally there are extra guards or other employees. In the larger counties there is an office, usually at the county courthouse, equipped and manned for the keeping of such records as are deemed necessary, for accounting, and sometimes for an engineering force.

There are certain tasks in connection with every gang that must be done either by hired men or by prisoners not under the gun. For the purpose of performing these tasks each camp has a small number of prisoners who are given a considerable amount of freedom. These prisoners are called trusties—usually pronounced *trustees* by supervisors and guards. The number of trusties is often determined by the number actually necessary to do the tasks requiring such freedom of movement. Some supervisors say that their policy is to have as few trusties as possible. Trusties serve quite often as "stool pigeons." A "stool pigeon," however, is not always a trusty. He may be a man under the gun. Apparently it is a quite general practice in these chain gangs for the supervisor to use this method of gaining information as to what goes on among the prisoners. There are, on the other hand, as has been pointed out in another chapter, a few camps where all the men are honor prisoners and there are other counties where the superintendent or supervisor attempts to place in the honor group as many of his men as he thinks can be trusted.

There is little uniformity as to hours of labor. In some counties ten hours is the maximum day. In others the working day is from daylight until dark.

Usually little machinery is used, because of the supposed necessity of working the men under guard and therefore in a compact squad. The work is, therefore, mainly of the pick and shovel sort. Unnecessarily crude and laborious methods, such as digging up trees instead of using dynamite, are used under an erroneous idea of economy. Sometimes the supervisor conceives it his first duty to keep the prisoners busy whether he gets the most roads built or not; so if it is a question of working the men at a loss to the county and letting the mules stand, or of working the mules to advantage and letting the men be at leisure, he thinks it his duty to work the men. It is not always practicable for the supervisor to remain in immediate charge of his men. In such cases he leaves the direction of the work in the hands of the guards. These guards, frequently, know very little about road building and have less knowledge of methods of handling men. As a rule, therefore, the county chain gang presents the appearance of a poorly organized and poorly directed group of laborers.

Chapter IV

TYPES OF COUNTY CONVICT ROAD CAMPS

THE provisions that have been made for the lodging and safekeeping of county prisoners sentenced to work on the roads follow no standardized construction comparable to the uniform types characteristic of jails and state prisons. Each county has apparently dealt with this problem of housing its prisoners with very little if any state supervision and has been guided for the most part by the desire to keep the prisoners securely with a minimum of expense. Before the days of automobile trucks, which have facilitated quick transportation to all parts of the county, it was necessary to move the camps frequently so that the men would always have convenient access to their work. This necessity has led to emphasis upon temporary and movable types of camps with the resulting tendency to get along with the cheapest and smallest quarters possible. With the development of better means of transportation there has come into favor in a few of the wealthier counties the plan of building a centrally located prison of a permanent type which serves as the lodging place of all the prisoners even though this involves many miles of travel to and from work.

In the majority of the counties using convict road labor the policy of moving camps from place to place is still looked upon as the most convenient method of making this labor supply available wherever needed. The fact also that such a policy avoids the necessity of making a large appropriation for a permanent prison has doubtless played an important part in the continued use of makeshift quarters of a temporary or movable type. At any rate, the apparent economic advantages of temporary camps have established them in popular favor and prevented any pronounced criticism of their defective structure and unsuitability as living quarters.

One of the most common types of movable prisons still in use in many of the counties, is the wooden or steel structure mounted on wheels which is popularly spoken of as the cage because of its resemblance to the cages in which wild animals are sometimes confined. In size, these so-called cages are usually 18 feet in length and 7 to 8 feet in height and width, designed to provide sleeping quarters for eighteen men. When constructed of steel, the roof, floor, front and rear ends of the cage consist of solid steel of sufficient thickness to provide security, while the two sides are enclosed by a close network of flat steel bars, thus providing plenty of ventilation. In bad weather, the sides of the cage are covered with a tarpaulin which gives protection against rain and cold, but interferes with ventilation and leaves the interior in darkness. The cage is entered through a solid steel door in the rear made secure by a padlock on the outside. The interior of the cage is fitted up with three three-decker bunks on either side of a narrow passage way about two feet wide. A small stove is crowded usually in the front end or middle of the cage and a kerosene lantern is swung from the ceiling. Each bunk is provided with blankets and a cheap mattress ordinarily not covered with a sheet. A night bucket and a pail of drinking water complete the equipment. When the cage is filled to capacity, there is no place for the men except in their bunks which are too low for a sitting posture. Since the men are locked in these cages not only at night, but on Saturday afternoons, Sundays, and on days when bad weather makes work impossible, it is obvious that such cramped quarters are particularly objectionable.

The older type of wooden cage is equipped in a similar manner with the exception that it is provided with one or two small windows for light and ventilation. Sometimes two cages are placed end to end with a small guard house between, so arranged that the night guard can command a view of both interiors. A better type of wooden cage is so constructed that by removing the adjacent sides two or more cages can be joined to form a more commodious building. In addition to the danger of fire, this wooden construction is lacking in security and makes necessary careful guarding or the use of chains to prevent escapes.

Since this type of portable prison provides only sleeping quarters for the prisoners, it is customary to locate the camp near some vacant farm buildings which can be used to house the guards and trusties and furnish a kitchen, mess hall, and storage facilities for prisoners and equipment. Through the selection of a camp site of this kind the county is able to provide living quarters for its convicts with a minimum of expense. The buildings, however, that can be rented for this purpose are ordi-

III. A County Convict Road Camp

Note the absence of windows, the horizontal plank under the eaves is on hinges and may be raised for ventilation.

IV. A County Convict Road Camp

Tarpaulin may be lowered to protect against the weather.

narily old and run down and entirely unsuited for use as a convict camp. The kitchen and mess hall are not screened, bathing facilities are lacking, and constant vigilance is necessary to deal with even the elementary problems of sanitation.

In some counties the type of quarters just described has been discarded in favor of portable buildings specially designed for use in a convict camp. Such buildings are usually of frame construction with the walls built in sections and bolted together so as to facilitate removal when the location of the camp is changed. These wall sections are made of uniform size, the usual dimensions being 18 feet long and 9 feet high, thus providing for a building 18 feet square or for a longer building by adding similar sections. With the roof also built in sections of suitable size and the floor boards so laid that they can be removed when the walls are taken down, the entire building can be transported to a new location with very little difficulty and with a minimum of depreciation. When the camp population is large enough to require a building of at least 18 x 54 feet for sleeping quarters, the interior is ordinarily divided into two bunk rooms at either end with a small guard room in the middle set off from the rest of the building by steel bar partitions. By means of this arrangement the two races can be given separate quarters and the guards have full view of the whole interior with no danger of being attacked by the prisoners. Since frame buildings of this kind cannot be made secure, it is customary to guard against escapes by chaining the prisoners at least during the night. This is accomplished by means of a heavy master chain to which are attached shorter chains fastened around the ankles of the prisoners. Since these buildings are heated by a stove and are highly inflammable, there is always the danger of fire with no quick means of releasing the prisoners in case of such an emergency.

The other buildings required by a portable camp are a kitchen and dining room, commissary, lodgings for the guards, stable, and shelter for the tools and equipment. In order to save expense these buildings are often of very cheap construction and may be poorly adapted to their purpose. The mess hall sometimes consists of a rough shed with open sides or may even be limited to rough tables and benches in the yard unprotected from the rain. In one of the counties in the eastern part of the state, it has been found practicable to use tents for the entire camp throughout the year. Because of the mild climate, substantially constructed and well heated buildings are not an absolute necessity from the point of view of health. On the whole the various types of portable convict camps, with the exception of the steel cages, do not differ widely from the usual road construction camps employing free labor. Nevertheless, they are entirely unsuited as places of detention for men who must be kept under guard, for security can be made possible only by the use of chains. The lack of a strong stockade is also one of their serious shortcomings, for without an enclosed yard in which the men can be given some freedom on Sundays and other days when they are not at work, they must be kept closely confined in their crowded sleeping quarters with no opportunity for exercise and recreation in the open air.

In the more populous counties where a convict road force of a hundred or more is maintained, the tendency is to build a centrally located prison of permanent type where all the county prisoners assigned to the roads are housed. During the early years of the county convict road system, a central prison did not seem practicable because of difficulties of transportation. It is significant that the first permanent prison for county convicts was built near Wilmington, the county seat of one of the smallest counties in the state, where the problem of transporting the convicts to and from their work was less serious than in the counties larger in area. This New Hanover County prison erected in 1914-15 is a two-story building constructed of concrete and has a capacity of 200 prisoners. Instead of adopting the cellular type of construction common in jails and state prisons, its designers chose a modified form of the congregate system with separate wards for the two races and smaller compartments for the segregation of the diseased and those assigned to solitary confinement for disciplinary purposes. One wing of the prison serves as a kitchen and a dining room large enough to seat all of the prisoners at one time. The building is equipped with modern lighting, heating, and plumbing, a distinctive feature being shower baths in each ward available for use of the prisoners at any time. Its substantial construction makes the use of chains unnecessary at night, and the high wire fence enclosing the prison yard provides a place for recreation and exercise on days when the prisoners are not engaged in their road work. While the prison has no farm of its own, its location adjoining the county poor farm enables the convicts to be assigned to farm work whenever this seems advisable, and the surplus products of the farm are readily accessible for use in the prison.

Within the past few years six other counties, [1] Guilford, Buncombe, Durham, Alamance, Rockingham, Edgecombe, and the Rocky Mount Road District have built permanent convict prisons of substantial materials, which conform more or less closely to the type of structure adopted at Wilmington. The most recent is the Durham County camp which was built in 1925 at a cost of $95,000, and has a capacity of 150 prisoners. This three-story structure, securely built of brick and surrounded by a heavy wire stockade, is perhaps the best planned prison of its kind in the state. On the first floor are the sleeping quarters of the convicts and the dining room and kitchen, while the second and third floors contain the hospital wards and the rooms for the superintendent and guards. As in Wilmington, the convicts sleep on cots in two large rooms, one for each race, separated by a guard room which affords full view of all the prisoners. Each ward opens into the common dining room where the whites and blacks eat at the same time, but at separate tables. The sleeping quarters have direct access to light and air by means of large windows made secure by steel bars. The building is heated by steam, and shower baths are provided for the prisoners in the basement.

[1] Bertie County has a permanent prison camp under construction.

V. New Hanover County Prison

An example of the better type of permanent quarters for the housing of county chain gangs.

VI. Union County Prison Camp

A type of wooden structure sometimes erected by counties unwilling to make a large capital outlay for buildings.

The Guilford County prison, which is built of native stone, has followed the plan of having separate one-story buildings for the sleeping quarters, dining room, kitchen, hospital, and quarters for the guards. Since it is believed that the county is too large to be served conveniently by one central prison, another permanent camp of frame construction is maintained in the southern part of the county.

The central prison of Buncombe County is located a few miles from Asheville and has a rock quarry near by where the convicts work when they are not out on the roads. The main building is two stories in height, and in its interior arrangement resembles the prisons already described. Separate dining rooms are provided for the two races, sleeping quarters are in the usual barracks style, and ample provision is made for the guards on the second floor. Located on a hillside overlooking the the French Broad River, this building constructed of native stone and well designed from an architectural point of view, makes the most pretentious appearance of all the county convict prisons.

In striking contrast to this somewhat elaborate prison is the much smaller and more simply constructed prison in Alamance County, which is an excellent example of how the problem of housing prisoners can be solved in a county where the comparatively small population does not justify a large expenditure of money. This prison located just outside the city of Graham near the county home consists of a group of one-story brick buildings very simple in appearance but securely constructed and equipped with modern heating and sanitary facilities. The main building provides the sleeping quarters for the convicts and a common mess hall. Other buildings, grouped near by, provide quarters for the guards and storage for the equipment and supplies. Erected at a cost of $21,-000 and affording accommodations for 40 prisoners, it has proven to be ample in size for the needs of Alamance County and represents perhaps what should be regarded as a minimum outlay for buildings by a county that adopts the county convict road system.

The remaining permanent camps constructed of substantial materials so as to provide security and safeguard health, are located in Edgecombe and Rockingham counties and the Rocky Mount Road District, and require no special description since they conform in general to the type of prison already discussed. Unfortunately, in at least two additional counties, Craven and Vance, the policy of a centrally located permanent prison has been adopted without provision for buildings suitable for this purpose. Constructed as they are of frame materials with inadequate facilities for sanitation and heating, they are in constant danger of fire and fail to meet the minimum requirements of a modern prison.

It is significant that after about forty years of experience with the county convict road system, less than ten counties in the state have built prisons of modern type for the housing of their convicts. Three-fourths of the counties that employ convicts on their roads still use makeshift quarters that are unsatisfactory from almost every point of view. The fact is that in many counties the convict road force is too small to justify the building of a suitable prison. Under these circumstances it would be preferable for such counties to send those convicted of crime to the state prison or to neighboring counties having properly equipped prison buildings. More than half the counties in the state are already following this policy of sending their convicts out of the county instead of using their labor in the construction and maintenance of their own roads. If suitable provision could be made for the more desperate and incompetent prisoners in the state prison or elsewhere, each county might organize an honor road camp for those prisoners who would need no further supervision than that ordinarily given to free labor. For the housing of such prisoners, temporary camps of the type used by road contractors for their employees would not be objectionable and could be maintained at small expense. Unless some plan can be worked out whereby the housing of the prisoners can be satisfactorily provided without too great expense, the county convict road system will prove untenable for all except those few counties that have a large number of prisoners.

Chapter V

PROBLEMS OF ADMINISTRATION: HEALTH AND SANITATION

THE maintenance of healthful living conditions in prisons, which even under the most favorable circumstances is a difficult matter, becomes a much more serious problem in the county convict road camps because standards vary widely in different counties and their scattered location interferes with adequate state supervision. When the county convict road work was first put into operation in the state, its management was vested in the county authorities with no special mention of the problem of health and sanitation. The first laws enumerating the duties of the county physician, who was employed by the county on a fee basis, required this official to attend the prisoners when sick but made no reference to the sanitary inspection of local prisons. [1] In 1893 when the State Board of Health was established, the county superintendent of health was given the responsibility of serving as sanitary inspector of the jail and county home. [2] It was not until 1901 that his duties were enlarged to include the sanitary inspection of the county convict camps with monthly reports to be made to the secretary of the State Board of Health as well as to the board of county commissioners. [3] Since at that time there were no full-time county

[1] N. C. Public Laws of 1879, chapter 117, section 5.
[2] N. C. Public Laws of 1893, chapter 214, section 5.
[3] N. C. Public Laws of 1901, chapter 247.

health officers, this part of their official duties was generally neglected. This lack of interest on the part of the county authorities in conditions in local prisons led in 1917 to the enactment of a law which gave the State Board of Health the "same supervision of all jails, county camps, or other places of confinement of county or city prisoners, in regard to method of construction, sanitary and hygienic care, as they have over the State prison." [4] This change of policy which turned over to the state full responsibility for the sanitary conditions in all local prisons and convict camps did not produce the desired results because the State Board of Health failed to give this work adequate attention and had no means of compelling the county officials to carry out its recommendations. A step toward meeting the difficulty was taken in 1925 when violation of the above law was made a misdemeanor punishable by fine or imprisonment or both in the discretion of the court. [5] At the same time the State Board of Health entered into a coöperative arrangement with the State Board of Charities and Public Welfare whereby both shared the expenses of a state sanitary inspector whose entire time was to be given to the enforcement of the state law concerning sanitary conditions in all the state, county and city prisons and convict camps.

During the period between 1917 and 1925 the state supervision of the sanitary conditions in county camps was placed in the hands of the sanitary inspectors of the State Board of Health, whose widespread duties made it impossible for them to

[4] N. C. Public Laws of 1917, chapter 286.
[5] N. C. Public Laws of 1925, chapter 163.

give more than incidental attention to these convict camps which were frequently difficult of access
because of their location in out-of-the-way places.
Fortunately their work in connection with the
prison camps during this period was supplemented
by members of the staff of the State Board of
Charities and Public Welfare, who, although not
trained sanitarians, were very vigorous in denounc-
ing the more obvious violations of sanitary regulations and did much to arouse public opinion on this
subject. It must be kept in mind, however, that
prior to 1925 the state authorities had no power to
enforce their recommendations when bad conditions were found in these county convict camps.

Under this new plan of state supervision of all
local prisons, the county health authorities act
simply as agents of the State Board of Health as far
as their responsibility for sanitary conditions of
convict camps is concerned. No longer are they required by law to make monthly inspections of local
prisons and report conditions to the county commissioners. Neither does the State Board of Health
require that such local inspections be made regularly, for in their detailed outline of duties assigned to
full-time county health officers working under a co-
operative plan with the State Board of Health no
mention is made of this particular task and no
routine reports are required covering either the
health of the prisoners or the sanitary conditions
of the camps.

For about one year following the passing of the
1925 law, the sanitary inspector of the State Board
of Health adopted the device of scoring the sanitary conditions of the convict camps on cards de-

vised for the purpose. At the present time instead of attempting to score each camp, the State Sanitary Inspector indicates his judgment after each visit by affixing to the premises an official card on which is printed in bold-type the words "Approved Prison Camp" or "Disapproved Prison Camp." When a camp is disapproved the county commissioners are given in writing a detailed statement of the conditions to be remedied and a later visit is made to see whether the recommended improvements have been carried out. The final recourse, in case bad conditions continue, is to the courts, a step that has not yet been taken although many violations of the law are of long standing with no apparent effort by the county authorities to improve conditions.

Under the present plan of state supervision, all rules and regulations governing the sanitary management of convict prison camps are drawn up and enforced by the State Board of Health. The existing regulations adopted in 1926, give detailed directions covering the whole field of camp sanitation including the health of prisoners, and set up high standards far beyond those attained in many of the counties. The use of the sanitary score card by the state inspector in 1925 represented the first serious attempt to determine the general status of sanitary conditions in county camps. Unfortunately the method of scoring was ill suited to present a fair picture of conditions in individual camps, for a camp filled with vermin and having an impure water supply could still secure a rating of 90 out of a possible 100. This defect in the scoring system does not, however, apply to separate items scored, as for example, the camp location, water supply, sewage disposal, etc. The following table sets forth the results of the inspection of fifty-three county camps during the year 1925, the percentage given indicating the average score of all the camps for the particular item listed. It should be kept in mind, of course, that this average includes the permanent well-kept camps, which would ordinarily receive a high score, and many badly managed temporary camps whose rating was in some instances extremely low.

Points Scored	Percentage
Location of camp	83
Construction, equipment, ventilation, etc.	73
Water Supply	71
Clothing	77
Bedding	64
Sewage Disposal	49
Vermin	67
Flies and Mosquitoes	54

Further concrete evidence concerning sanitary conditions in county convict camps is available in the files of the State Board of Charities and Public Welfare, where the reports of the state sanitary inspector under the new plan of administration are kept. The following excerpts from recent official reports and letters to county commissioners give a vivid picture of conditions that are frequently found.

Inspection of this camp would show that from a standpoint of sanitation, there is nothing possible to do except erect new buildings. No toilets have been built and woods above buildings have been used for toilets.

Drainage from these woods comes directly through camp and sanitary conditions are generally bad. Impossible to screen buildings in the shape they are in.

You are hereby notified that your convict prison camp is violating the law as follows: Garbage cans are not provided with lids; the kitchen is not properly screened; food is exposed to flies and dirt; the beds are very dirty, need new mattresses and covers; prisoners are not provided with night shirts; sewage disposal is unsanitary; the sleeping tent canvas is rotten and does not prevent rain from entering thus wetting prisoners and beds.

The following items need attention in prison camp Number 2: Food exposed to flies and dirt; prisoners' beds need improving, wires are broken, bed linen and clothing need to be aired; the privy is not constructed according to the approved plan of the State Board of Health; a few more tubs are needed for the prisoners to take their baths; the cages need to be painted and thoroughly cleaned.

The camp needs improvement along the following lines: Sewerage arrangements in bad order, has very disagreeable odor; water supply contaminated; some beds very dirty, vermin present, screens need repairing, ventilation poor; a thorough cleansing of walls and floors with hot water, soap, and scrub brush would be very beneficial.

The water samples collected at the prison camp show by analysis at the State Laboratory of Hygiene, B-coli present in 10 c.c. of samples. This well is an open well and water is drawn up for use with a bucket and chain system, which affords an excellent opportunity for polluting the water.

Stables need to be cleaned and manure removed to prevent fly breeding. Some of the beds do not have bed covers or sheets. The prisoners are not provided with night shirts and sleep in their work clothes. Proper screening and the use of anti-fly measures for the kitchen neglected. Some of the table ware is covered with rust. The privy needs to be made fly proof. I will thank you to have these violations corrected at once.

The housing conditions at the camp are very inadequate and are far from the requirements of the rules and regulations governing the management of convict prison camps in North Carolina. The old cages, kitchen, and sleeping quarters have depreciated until they are about useless. I doubt very much whether they could be moved without tearing to pieces. You recall that I told you while in your office that the conditions made the sanitary score for the camp very low. I hope your Board will be ready to take up this matter and make some arrangements for improving the camp at its next meeting.

The following violations of the sanitary regulations have been found in your camp. Location of the camp bad. The building not fire proof. It is perilous to keep those prisoners locked in that wooden building with oil, etc., near. No provisions for bathing or toilets. Beds and bed clothing very dirty. The building poorly arranged for air and sunshine. No seats to sit on. No spittoons. Heating arrangement bad.

The following is a list of the needed improvements for your convict prison camp. Provide sufficient underclothing and night shirts for the prisoners; provide proper bedding for the prisoners,—sheets, covers, and mattresses; provide individual wash basin, towels and soap; provide adequate tubs for bathing; provide approved sanitary privies; provide dining place for prisoners other than sleeping quarters; isolate syphilitic prisoners and do not allow them to eat or sleep with the other prisoners.

These official records of violations of the sanitary regulations present an unpleasant but vivid picture of conditions that still exist in some of the worst convict camps. For the most part such conditions are found only in the temporary camps located in counties where the public has been indifferent to the health and welfare of prisoners. The well built, permanent camps that are taking the place of the older movable types, ordinarily comply with the state sanitary regulations and provide decent and healthful living quarters. The chief problem seems to be the development of a public opinion that will insist on higher standards of prison construction and management. A few years ago, one of the most populous counties in the state gained unpleasant notoriety because of public exposure of bad conditions existing in its prison camps. The county board of charities and public welfare ably supported by an influential local newspaper kept the public informed about the situation with the result that the county authorities finally appropriated the funds necessary for the construction of a modern prison of approved type. At the present time three counties, each sufficiently populous to maintain a convict road force of about one hundred and fifty, continue to use steel cages and temporary wooden camps so constructed that it is impossible to conform to the sanitary standards set up by the state. As a matter of fact, at least three-fourths of all the county prison camps occupy quarters of such a nature that it is exceedingly difficult if not impracticable to maintain healthful living conditions for prisoners even under the best management.

Without doubt, the whole problem of convict camp sanitation is complicated by the continued prevalence in many counties of the traditional idea that punishment must necessarily be harsh, severe, and painful. If it is pointed out that a convict camp is full of vermin and improperly heated and ventilated, the public is likely to respond that this is regrettable but still nothing to be greatly disturbed about, for it would defeat the purpose of punishment to make prisons comfortable places in which to live. As long as such an attitude of mind prevails, it is extremely difficult to enforce existing laws and regulations designed to safeguard the health of county convicts. Inspection may be made regularly by the state sanitary inspector and recommendations offered looking toward improvement, but it is difficult to remedy bad conditions if neither the county officials nor the general public see any reason why better standards should be maintained.

In view of the low standards of hygiene and sanitation in many of the convict camps, a high mortality rate among the prisoners would seem to be an inevitable result. Unfortunately, accurate data on this point cannot be given because of the general lack of adequate medical records. While medical treatment of prisoners confined in county convict camps has been, during the past 25 years, one of the prescribed duties of county physicians, it has not been customary to keep records of the work done. Following the enactment of the law of 1917 [6] which required the county health authorities to submit reports to the State Board of Health concerning the health of prisoners when requested to do so, the State Board of Health prepared a schedule for a monthly report on the condition of convicts covering such items as the number of prisoners ill during the month, the most important

---

[6] *N. C. Public Laws of* 1917, chapter 286, section 10.

causes of illness, and the total number of work days lost on account of sickness. The counties, however, failed to comply with this request to submit such reports and the State Board of Health took no further steps to secure information concerning the health of the county convicts. At the present time the required report of the full time county health officer to the State Board of Health includes a statement of the number of visits made to the convict camp to give medical treatment but gives no facts about the health conditions found.

Within recent years the state laws dealing with the health of convicts have emphasized the necessity of diagnosing and treating all cases of venereal disease and tuberculosis. In order that such cases may be discovered promptly, the law requires that the county physician make a thorough physical examination of every prisoner committed to the convict camp within 48 hours after his admission. [7] If venereal disease is found, the regulations of the State Board of Health provide that "all prisoners who have syphilis, chancroid, or gonorrhea in an infectious stage, shall be isolated to the extent of using separate bathing equipment, eating and drinking utensils, and bed clothing, Wearing apparel, towels, and bed clothing used by such prisoners shall be handled and laundered separately from that of other prisoners and shall be boiled in laundering. All such prisoners shall be constantly under the care of the physician in charge until rendered non-infectious." [8] In case of tuberculosis,

---

[7] *Consolidated Statutes of North Carolina*, section 7216.
[8] *Convict Prison Camps*, State Board of Health, Raleigh, N. C., 1925.

the prisoner may be sent to the criminal ward of the State Tuberculosis Sanatorium.

Available evidence indicates that the law requiring a routine physical examination is not generally complied with except perhaps in cases where outward signs of disease or the physical weakness of the prisoner seem to make such an examination necessary. Under such circumstances it is extremely doubtful whether the superintendents of the convict camps are always aware of the physical disabilities of their prisoners. Furthermore, very few if any of the temporary convict camps possess facilities for even the amount of isolation required by the State Board of Health in the case of venereal disease. One county stands out in striking contrast to the others by providing an entirely separate camp for venereal cases. Since a sufficient number of such cases were found in this county to establish a camp comprising one-fourth of all their prisoners, it would seem that where no isolation camps are maintained, a promiscuous mingling of diseased and non-diseased would be inescapable. The only exceptions to this may be found in the permanent camps which usually have rooms set aside for hospital purposes. But the small number of prisoners confined in these hospital wards or held at the county jail for medical treatment seems to warrant the conclusion that the only prisoners ordinarily isolated are those in whom the disease has made such inroads as to incapacitate them for work. As far as tuberculosis is concerned, the lack of a careful medical examination prevents the discovery of the disease in its incipient stages and the county authorities are not likely to discover the need for sanatorium treatment until the weak condition of the prisoners makes their work unprofitable. Last year out of the six thousand prisoners [9] committed during that period to the county convict camps, nineteen were transferred to the State Tuberculosis Sanatorium.

The following excerpt from an official report of a county board of charities and public welfare to the board of county commissioners calls attention to the lack of adequate medical care of prisoners in one of the leading counties of the state three years ago.

We report to you, upon evidence that warrants us in finding as facts, that prisoners confined to beds because of sickness have been left unattended for a half a day or longer at a time, with no one to give such a one a drink of water or any medicine. One negro, who went to the camp as a strong man, is a physical wreck, because of two accidents and indifferent treatment following them. Another negro was permitted to lie on his cot and have fits with no one to minister to him, until he was mercifully carried to the county home and permitted to escape. Men in the two camps are now being worked who complain of being physically unable to do so, and who declare they have not been given a thorough physical examination. If this is doubted, we suggest that it be tested by having a physical examination of some of those men, including cooks, by any physician of the county who is an examiner for any reputable life insurance company. We are not physicians and cannot say ourselves how this may be, but the complaints of prisoners as to medical treatment and lack

---

[9] No exact figures are available concerning the number of commitments to the county camps during any one year. The number given is an estimate made by the State Board of Charities and Public Welfare on the basis of incomplete reports from 31 counties.

of examinations are too overwhelming and consistent to
be ignored by your board.

In the investigation which followed this report,
sufficient evidence of neglect and incompetency on
the part of the county physician was brought forth
to bring upon him severe criticism, and was followed
by his resignation. One particularly flagrant case
referred to in the above report was that of a Negro
convicted of a petty crime, who was treated by the
county physician for epilepsy and later was regarded by him as a malingerer although his physical condition incapacitated him for labor on the
roads. Following this man's escape from the county
home to which he had been transferred, his case
came to the attention of the State Board of Charities and Public Welfare, under whose direction a
thorough physical examination was made which
revealed a Wassermann reaction of three plus with
a definite diagnosis of neuro-syphilis. A letter from
the State Commissioner of Public Welfare to the
county commissioners commenting on this case included these significant statements:

The diagnosis of the case shows not only that the
man has syphilis but that the disease has attacked the
nervous centers. The fact is that the man is a hopelessly
sick man physically and mentally. His mental condition, we suspect, is probably responsible both for his
conduct while on the chain gang and for the crime for
which he was imprisoned. If a careful examination of
this prisoner had been made when he was sent to your
camp his real condition would have been disclosed.
He should then have been separated from other prisoners and treated for syphilis. When it was known
that his mind was affected by the disease, no one who

understood the working of this particular form of insanity would have been surprised at the untrue statements that the fellow made about his past life, or that he should pretend to be afflicted in other ways than he was.

It should be noted that this failure to comply with the law requiring adequate diagnosis and medical treatment of prisoners occurred in one of the more populous and progressive counties where a full time health officer was employed. The following extract from an official report of a member of the staff of the State Board of Public Welfare gives an unpleasant picture of the lack of medical care of prisoners in a temporary camp a few years ago which may be regarded as representative of the worst conditions found only in counties where public health standards are low:

Three of these men were sick men, another one the cook and the fifth a man assisting around the camp. Two of the sick men were confined in one cage, the third one was in an old house that is used as a bunk house at night instead of the cages. The two sick men in the regulation cages have tuberculosis. They have each been in bed a month; one has ten months still to serve, the other eleven. No sleeping garments are provided them. They have on the regular convict stripes. The third man has running syphilitic sores on his legs. The tubercular patients have not receptacles to expectorate in, consequently they use the ground, the floor of their cage, and anything that is convenient. There are no screens in the cages or in the kitchen to protect the food. Flies are swarming everywhere. The kitchen is only a short distance from the cage where the sick men are confined; and even nearer the cage than the kitchen is a block of wood on which meat is chopped. When we visited the camp the meat was lying on the block of wood exposed to the flies and dust. The filth of the bedding and the sleeping quarters of this camp is indescribable. The sick negroes were asked how frequently they got clean bed clothes. One negro replied that he had been in bed a month and no clean bedding had been given him. From the appearance of the bed I could well believe this to be true.[10]

The fact that the county health authorities would permit such conditions to exist in a county convict camp gives ample justification for the recent efforts on the part of the state to keep these camps under closer supervision. Without doubt too many county physicians have been derelict in their duty of examination and medical treatment of prisoners. Even at the present time the impossibility of securing accurate information from the county departments of health concerning the health of prisoners seems to indicate their failure to carry on this phase of their work in a systematic and efficient manner. When we go a step farther and make inquiries about the mental health and status of county convicts, we enter a field that is still almost completely neglected. The following case reported by the State Board of Charities and Public Welfare illustrates the present indifference to the significance of mental disease in the county convict camps:

---

[10] *Biennial Report*, North Carolina State Board of Charities and Public Welfare, 1920-22, p. 85.

Last Christmas a Negro who was ordinarily an industrious and dependable worker—a fireman at a saw-mill—under the influence of whiskey went on a rampage which landed him in a chain gang. Here he refused to work on the ground that he had wronged no one and it would be sinful for him to work. He was subjected to every form of torture that the superintendent of the camp could devise. He was beaten; he was chained in uncomfortable positions for long periods; he was chained behind a truck for a whole day—sometimes forced to walk, sometimes dragged. No treatment forced him to work. He was finally released. He went back to work. Several months passed. He had saved more than a hundred dollars of his wages. A few weeks ago, after calking a boiler on a hot day, he again drank some whiskey and perhaps also some liniment, and again went wild. He was again sent to a chain gang, this time in a different county. Here he was first beaten and then coaxed but still refused to work. Finally it occurred to those in charge that he had been insane all the while.

Upon examination by an alienist it was found that he was a victim of dementia praecox and suffered from an hallucination that God appeared to him and told him that it was sinful for him to work. He is now in the State Hospital for the Negro insane, but it was more or less of an accident that he was not killed before his condition was discovered.[11]

Incidents of this nature could be multiplied which afford substantial evidence of the lack of medical care and attention under present methods of administering county convict camps. Recently, through the efficient work of the state sanitary inspector of prisons marked improvement is notice-

---

[11] *Public Welfare Progress*, August 1924, June 1925.

able in the observance of sanitary laws and regulations. It is unfortunate that the State Board of Health does not go a step farther and give close supervision to the work of county physicians who are required by law to look after the health of county prisoners. As long as no routine reports concerning the health of prisoners are made either to the county authorities or the State Board of Health, it may be assumed that this part of the official duties of the county physician is done perfunctorily and with varying degrees of efficiency in the different counties.

Chapter VI

PROBLEMS OF ADMINISTRATION:
MAINTENANCE OF DISCIPLINE

NO PRISON official has a more difficult task than the man in charge of the county chain gang. To him are sent a heterogeneous group of offenders. He must deal with misdemeanants and felons, with first offenders and recidivists, with the feebleminded, the insane and psychopathic, and the normal, with the diseased and the well. And no one has thought it worth while to collect the available facts about these prisoners, and inform him so that he may know within what class they will probably fall. He must work all these with facilities and under conditions favorable only for working honor prisoners who are also physically fit for the heaviest manual labor. He is generally without strong walls, even for confinement at night, and he has few tasks fit for physical weaklings. With no knowledge of other than physical restraints, he is driven to rely on chains and guns. Unwilling to allow men to spend their time in idleness, he knows no choice but to set men at tasks to which they may not be physically equal.

The prison exists primarily for the protection of society. The men who are sentenced to the chain gang will after a few months, or a very few years at most, again go back into society. On any theory of punishment other than of vengeance or of deterrence, the chain gang can justify its right to existence only when officials placed in charge of the prisoners are men of character, skilled in methods of controlling men by inspiring respect. Such men among chain gang officials are very rare. Usually the men in immediate charge of county prisoners working on the roads are by character and training unfit to have any such authority over other men as is thought necessary in the typical prison. "Unfortunate, ignorant men, strained beyond capacity, incapable of fortitude and needing some outlet and escape for a fruitless, barren existence, impose their wills upon other men more unfortunate and more helpless." [1] Quite often both the supervisor, as the ranking official in charge of the county prison camp is most frequently called, and the guards, who are usually not merely guards but also general assistants to the supervisor, are in standards of conduct and ideals of life but little above the average prisoner.

In one county in the state in recent years the supervisor of the chain gang was convicted of receiving stolen goods, from a trusty on the gang! [2] The superintendent in immediate charge of the prisoners in another county at the present time was recently driven from the county seat of the same county, along with his wife, on the charge of keeping a "disorderly house." His chief assistant is generally known as a former bootlegger. When Tannenbaum asked a supervisor of more than average intelligence what the guards do on their one night a week off, the supervisor answered, "Oh, we

---

[1] Frank Tannenbaum: *Darker Phases of the South*, p. 74.
[2] *North Carolina Supreme Court Reports*, 172:896, *State vs. Mincher.*

run after the girls." [3] In November, 1925, a supervisor who had been in charge of a prison camp in
one of the piedmont counties for several years was
arrested in Thomasville, N. C., with a load of
liquor. Two prisoners, trusties, were with him. [4]
On March 5, 1926, L. G. Whitley, inspector of
prisons for the State Board of Charities and Public
Welfare and the State Board of Health reported:
"I note in today's paper that one of the guards in
Sampson County has been indicted for violating
the liquor law. . . . That makes the fourth one
within the past few weeks over the State to be indicted." [5] Instances of violations of law by those in
charge of county convicts are numerous enough,
it seems, to warrant the conclusion that no great
gulf exists in many instances between the prisoner
and the official in charge of him.

The State Board of Charities and Public Welfare, commenting on this general theme in 1922,
said:

The most common wage for a guard is around $50
per month. Such a wage, coupled with the class of
work that a guard on a typical chain gang must do does
not often attract the type of man who is fit to have
charge of other men. The guard is usually without even
an elementary education, often practically illiterate.
He is ignorant, of course, of any method of controlling
men except by force. The supervisor is often a man who,
on account of a little superior intelligence, or devotion to

[3] Tannenbaum: *Darker Phases of the South*, p. 78.
[4] *Greensboro Daily News*, November 30, 1925.
[5] Letter in files of North Carolina State Board of Charities
and Public Welfare.

duty, or mere length of service, has been promoted from the ranks of the guards.[6]

The biennial report of the State Board of Charities and Public Welfare for the years 1922-24 quotes the statement of the preceding report as to the character of guards and supervisors, and adds; "There has been no general change in the type of men employed. There continue to be a few camps that stand out in sharp contrast to the others. There are a few supervisors who are eager to learn of better methods of handling men." [7]

The public does not demand that the official in charge of the chain gang shall be of a higher type. "The management has heretofore largely merely reflected the general attitude toward prisoners, that is, one of careless indifference—that anything was too good but nothing too bad." [8]

"The most hopeless thing about the whole situation," says the State Commissioner of Public Welfare, "is that the public generally accepts such conditions as a matter of course." In support of this statement, the following excerpts from the report of a grand jury are given:

We sent a committee of three to inspect the team camp of the convict force and found that the teams were in excellent condition, well sheltered and well cared for. (The men at this camp are not mentioned.)

---

[6] *Biennial Report*, North Carolina State Board of Charities and Public Welfare, 1920-22, p. 83.

[7] *Biennial Report*, North Carolina State Board of Charities and Public Welfare. 1922-24, p. 68.

[8] R. F. Beasley, Commissioner of Public Welfare, *Biennal Report*, North Carolina State Board of Charities and Public Welfare, 1918, p. 11.

The grand jury visited the convict camp No. 1 and talked with the prisoners, and they said that they were well cared for and had no cause for complaint. The sanitary conditions surrounding the camp were good.

The report of the Commissioner continues:

This is the camp in which the bedding is described above as "simply a bundle of filthy rags." Moreover, just before this visit was made two prisoners had been beaten in violation of the law, until their backs were blistered. If the grand jury was composed of men of ordinary intelligence, they knew about that beating. The probability is that they were good men, but that they had always been accustomed to regard brutality as a necessary part of and filth as inseparable from a prison camp. In this they were not different from the average group in the average county in the State.[9]

When public sentiment was finally aroused to the point of forcing the resignation of a supervisor in one of the counties of the state, after a career of brutality had culminated in the killing of a prisoner, he found no difficulty in securing a job in a near-by county where he remained in charge of the prisoners until his death, which was hastened, report says, by heavy drinking. In 1925 a chain gang official, locally called the "walking boss," with a reputation of long standing for brutality, was dismissed by order of a Superior Court judge and indicted for murder. Almost immediately, and apparently without difficulty, he secured a position as guard in a camp fifty miles from the one from which he had been dismissed. In almost every case where

---

[9] North Carolina State Board of Charities and Public Welfare, *Biennial Report*, 1920-1922, p. 86.

a superintendent or supervisor of a county chain gang has been charged with a crime in connection with his treatment of prisoners, he has had the support of the county that employed him. The case of the supervisor already referred to who was convicted of receiving stolen goods is one in point. Two years before this he was charged with having flogged a prisoner. The supervisor was indicted, convicted of an assault, and sentenced to imprisonment. He appealed, but the findings of the lower court were confirmed. But his backing in the county was such that a pardon was secured before he had served a single day of the sentence. Two years later he was convicted of receiving stolen goods. Again he appealed, and again the lower court was sustained. A second time a pardon was secured without his having paid any part of the penalty imposed. Numerous other cases can be cited, one notable one still pending in the courts. The public conscience has been aroused only to the point where it feels in a vague way that the county is being held responsible, but not to the point where it is willing to accept such responsibility. The result is a defensive reaction.

The state law provides that, "The convicts sentenced to hard labor on the public roads . . . shall be under the control of the county authorities, and the county authorities have power to enact all needful rules and regulations for the successful working of convicts upon the public roads." [10] The Supreme Court has held that "it is the duty of the county commissioners to prescribe rules regulating

---

[10] *Consolidated Statutes of North Carolina,* section 1361.

the punishment to be given to refractory prisoners, stating the kind and *quantum* of punishment, to what breach of discipline applicable, and by whom to be inflicted, which duty they cannot delegate; their order that the road superintendent be authorized to use such means as he deems necessary to enforce obedience cannot be construed to authorize the infliction of corporal punishment." [11] In *Public Welfare Progress* for September 1, 1922, appears this paragraph:

Two weeks ago a letter was addressed by the State Board of Charities and Public Welfare to the chairman of the board of county commissioners in every county maintaining a chain gang, asking for a copy of the printed rules for the management of the prison camps in his county. Two counties have sent typewritten copies of rules enacted by the commissioners. A third sends a statement dictated by the superintendent of its prison camp. Only one of the typewritten copies of rules submitted gives the date of adoption.

In the biennial report of the State Board of Charities and Public Welfare, 1924, it is stated that "very few counties have enacted such rules."

The making of specific rules for the control of prisoners is a difficult task for a board of county commissioners, or county road commission, to which the duty seems to have been delegated in a number of counties. They know little of the problem which confronts them. When they attempt such rules, the result, apart from those dealing with matters of routine, is often a set of regulations con-

---

[11] *North Carolina Supreme Court Reports*, 172:896, *State vs. Mincher.*

cerning things of rather minor importance. The following from a list of nineteen are quoted in *Public Welfare Progress:*

> 1. Profane and vulgar language is prohibited at all times.
> 4. No smoking is permitted during working hours.
> 12. No food shall be wasted.
> 15. No trading between convicts and those having them in charge shall be indulged in.

The punishments prescribed for these offenses follow:

> For the first violation, the convict or prisoner shall be placed in solitary confinement in a dark cell for a space of forty-eight hours and shall be furnished during said period bread and water only.
> For a second violation the convict or prisoner shall be deemed incorrigible and shall be whipped or flogged.[12]

For such petty offenses the county official can think of no punishment except physical torture. Think of applying the standard of conduct prescribed in these rules to all the officials and employees about the courthouse. And why was it considered necessary to prescribe severe punishment for the prisoner to keep the superintendent and guards from trading with him?

From another county comes the following:

> Resolved that: If any prisoner sentenced to work on the county roads of . . . county, or serving a sentence on the chain gang or county roads of . . . county shall infringe or disobey the lawful rules of the superintendent

---

[12] *Public Welfare Progress*, September 1, 1922.

of roads and gangs, or guards, or shall refuse to work as and when directed by the superintendent of roads, or by the guard in charge, such prisoner shall be sentenced in the following manner:

The guard shall report the conduct to the superintendent of the gang. The superintendent shall report it to the county physician or health officer. They shall set a time and place to punish such prisoner. The punishment shall be inflicted by the superintendent of the gang in the presence of the county physician or health officer, by whipping according to the circumstances of the case.[13]

Here whipping is prescribed for every offense. It is needless to point out that the rules do not conform to the law as interpreted by the Supreme Court in *State vs. Mincher.*

A number of cases of extremely brutal beating of prisoners are to be found in the files of the State Board of Charities and Public Welfare. Several of these are supplemented by court records. In two well-known cases a prisoner died within a few hours after being flogged; and in a third case two prisoners died also within a few hours. In each case the county physician found that the prisoner died from causes other than the beating he had received. The two last named, the physician said, died from sunstroke. In 1925 in a chain gang with a long standing reputation for inhuman treatment of prisoners, a prisoner died under the blows of the guard who was beating him. The prompt and vigorous action of the Judge who happened to be presiding over the Superior Court of the county at the time, sent the guard to the state prison.

---

[13] Files of North Carolina State Board of Charities and Public Welfare.

Subsequently, after an examination, a psychologist pronounced this guard sub-normal mentally. The repeated occurrence of even occasional cases of such extreme brutality seems to warrant the conclusion reached by Judge Clark, after a study of the first two cases referred to above:

Such punishment as was here inflicted was never necessary, and to permit the whipping of convicts in any case is to permit it to the extent and in the manner and according to the temper and unrestricted will of the overseer, for the only witnesses are the cowed fellow convicts who fear a similar punishment at any hour.[14]

As to the legality of flogging as a method of punishment under any circumstances there is difference of judicial opinion. In the case of *State vs. Mincher* already referred to, and in another one a little earlier,[15] Chief Justice Clark took the position that flogging is in all cases illegal. The constitution provides that the only punishments for crime shall be fine, imprisonment with or without hard labor, and death. There is no general state law prescribing or permitting the flogging of prisoners in county prisons or chain gangs in the state. On this point Judge Clark writes:

Prior to the constitution of 1868 corporal punishment was allowed, such as branding for manslaughter, cutting off the ears for perjury, and whipping and setting in the stocks for larceny, and other crimes, but in no case without the verdict of a jury of twelve im-

---

[14] *North Carolina Supreme Court Reports*, 172:895, *State vs. Mincher*.
[15] *North Carolina Supreme Court Reports*, 166:272, *State vs. Nipper*.

partial men rendered in open court and the sentence of a judge. The advancing civilization of the age required that corporal punishment even in such cases and with such safeguards should be abolished, which was done by the Constitution, Article 11, Section 1. This removed from our statute book all possibility of whipping or other corporal punishment even by the verdict of a jury, with the guaranteed right of the benefit of counsel and the judgment of a court. Certainly it could not have been contemplated that whipping should be inflicted without a verdict, without a trial of any kind, and without the sentence of a court. Such punishment without a jury trial and judgment was unknown to the law, even in the most barbarous days of the common law. It needed no Constitution and no statute to forbid its imposition by the arbitrary act of an officer, and no statute has since authorized the infliction of whipping, branding or cutting off ears in any case, and the defendant here had no right to inflict either.

Further, in the course of his opinion, after citing precedent for such a course, he says:

Even if the common law had ever recognized the right of an official in charge of prisoners to whip them at his own pleasure and to any extent he wishes (which it never did) and if, further, the Constitution had not forbidden the infliction of such punishment, even under authority of a verdict by a jury and sentence by a judge, still the court in response to the sentiment of a more enlightened and juster age would need no authority further than to say, "We have advanced from that barbarism."

He even extends the responsibility to include the county officials who have general supervision over the prisoners:

I think that if the county commissioners had given the defendant the power to inflict such punishment as this they would have been responsible, both by indictment and by civil action for damages; and that if such punishment had been previously inflicted so often that by reasonable supervision the county commissioners should have heard of it and had not removed the overseer and caused him to be prosecuted, they would have been equally responsible both by indictment and by an action for damages by the party aggrieved for willful omission and neglect of duty.

The majority of the Supreme Court of the state have never concurred in the advanced stand taken by Chief Justice Clark. Flogging of prisoners has, therefore, not been outlawed.[16] In 1923 Governor Morrison, after an agitation for two years by the North Carolina Conference for Social Service and the State Board of Charities and Public Welfare, ordered the use of the lash discontinued in the state prison system. At the same time he requested the county commissioners of the various counties to abolish it in the county chain gangs, but they did not see fit to do so.[17]

Within the last few months four Superior Court judges, and one of them, at least, repeatedly over a period of two years or more, have taken positive stands against flogging, agreeing substantially with the position taken by Judge Clark.[18]

---

[16] In the most recent case, *State vs. Revis*, the Supreme Court upheld the constitutionality of the Buncombe County local law which specifically confers the power to flog as a means of discipline. The question of the right of county officials to whip in the absence of any law specifically permitting such punishment was not before the court.   *South Eastern Reporter*, Vol. 136, No. 6, February 26, 1927, pp. 346-350.

[17] North Carolina State Board of Charities and Public Welfare, *Biennial Report*, 1922-24, pp. 67-68.

[18] *Public Welfare Progress*, August, 1926.

Not all supervisors, however, rely entirely on whipping. On the subject of punishments for the purpose of enforcing discipline a report of the State Board of Charities and Public Welfare says:

Governor Morrison, in the summer of 1923, requested county authorities to abolish the lash. Of the thirty counties reporting, seven reported flogging used as a punishment. It is known to the State Board of Charities and Public Welfare that several other counties that did not report at all, or not on this item, practice flogging. The counties reporting flogging are Forsyth with three floggings, one white man and two Negroes, in seven months; Guilford, two white men, four Negro men, and six Negro women in four months; Lenoir four Negroes, in two months; Robeson, three Negroes in five months; Rowan, sixteen white men and sixteen Negroes, in seven months; Sampson, one Negro, in three months; and Wayne, three white men and twelve Negroes in ten months. The total number of prisoners flogged in the seven counties is twenty-two white men, sixty-four Negro men and six Negro women. The Negro women were employed in connection with the county home. They were flogged by the chain gang foreman. The offense assigned in four cases is "fighting and cursing," and in the other two, "misconduct in patients' dining room."

In addition to flogging the following punishments are reported: Confinement in a dark cell, twelve cases; loss of time gained for good behavior, sixty-eight cases; other punishments, seventeen cases. The last group includes chaining at night, putting in double shackles, to eat corn bread and water two days, and "made to eat fish raw." The confinement in dark cells ranges from thirty-six to forty-eight hours. Offenses for which prisoners were punished include: cursing; fighting; not working; misconduct; "violation of rules"; stealing fish; stealing sugar, meal, etc. and making beer; threatening superintendent. The man who stole fish was made to eat raw fish; the man who attempted to make a run of home brew was flogged; the man who threatened the superintendent was put on bread and water for two days. These three offenses occurred, of course, in different counties. The last, which was the most serious offense reported, occurred in one of the best disciplined camps in the State. The superintendent considered bread and water for two days sufficient for the preservation of discipline. [19]

Reports in the files of the State Board of Charities and Public Welfare by the state inspector on thirty-seven of the forty-seven counties which now maintain chain gangs, show that thirty of these counties admit the use of flogging as a means of discipline. The same number use chains, some for most of the prisoners and some for only a few. The counties that are reported as still whipping prisoners are Alamance, Anson, Beaufort, Buncombe, Cabarrus, Columbus, Craven, Davidson, Durham, Forsyth, Gaston, Granville, Guilford, Halifax, Henderson, Johnston, Lenoir, Mecklenburg, Nash, Rocky Mount Road District, New Hanover, Robeson, Rockingham, Rowan, Sampson, Scotland, Union, Wake, and Wayne. Chatham says that it has not flogged in a "long time," and Washington has whipped none in twelve months. In neither case is it stated that this method of punishment has been definitely abandoned.

Chains are used both as a precaution against escape and as punishment. For these purposes three devices are used—"single shackles," "double

[19] North Carolina State Board of Charities and Public Welfare, *Biennial Report*, 1922-1924, pp. 68-69.

shackles," and "spikes." Each of these may need a word of explanation:

Single Shackle. An iron or steel band is placed around the left ankle, usually riveted on by the blacksmith; sometimes secured by a small padlock. To this is attached a chain about three feet long, the loose end of which is fastened to the prisoner's belt when he is at work. At night the chain is attached to a rod or "bull-chain" running through the bunk-house or tent at the foot of the beds.

Double Shackles. To a cuff riveted around each ankle are attached the ends of a chain usually about twenty inches long, which thus ties the legs together and limits the length of the step to that of the chain. There is also the three-foot chain used in securing the prisoner at night, which in this case is often detachable, so that the prisoner does not wear it when at work.

Spike. This is a sharp pointed iron instrument resembling an ordinary pick with the "eye" riveted around the ankle. Its two prongs, each ten inches in length and bent slightly upwards, extend out from the ankle both in front and behind. Since it is worn constantly, it is not merely a hindrance to free movement but is very uncomfortable when the prisoner is lying down.

Neither shackles nor spikes when they are riveted on, and this is the usual method, can be removed until they are cut off by the blacksmith. The weight of the chains used varies from that of very light trace chains to that of light log chains. The writer has seen spikes used in only two counties in

North Carolina, and within the last two years in only one, Mecklenburg. [20]

As has already been suggested there are counties where these primitive methods of discipline are not in use. There are still others where they are used only in extreme cases. The following account of the successful use of more humane methods of discipline is taken from the biennial report of the State Board of Charities and Public Welfare:

Two counties have shown that brutality is not necessary in prison discipline. Up against the Brushy Mountains, Alexander County, for a year or more, has been conducting an interesting experiment in prison discipline. She found herself with a small group of prisoners that she had difficulty in finding a place for in other counties as had been her custom. It would be expensive for the county to run a chain gang, but Mr. C. W. Mayberry, chairman of the board of county commissioners, decided that by establishing the proper personal contacts with the men he could work them without guards. He determined to try out his plan. Two men escaped soon after the camp started. One was recaptured and sent to Rowan County. The other, an old man who was not able to work much and could not be kept employed, has not been recaptured. Since then there has been no trouble. When seen a few months ago

---

[20] A recent inspection of the three camps in the county reveals that the camps, especially the bunks on which the men sleep, are filthy; that prisoners are given a bath only once in two weeks; that the majority of the men are worked under the gun and in chains; that these chains are unusually heavy and that in addition some of the prisoners are weighted with heavy spikes on one or sometimes both ankles; that on Sundays the men are not only locked in and under guard, but are chained to their bunks; that the guards in general appearance, apparent intellect, and in attitude towards the prisoners, rank low; that no provision has been made for regular religious instruction of the prisoners. *Agricultural Mecklenburg and Industrial Charlotte*, 1926, Charlotte Chamber of Commerce, Charlotte, N. C., p. 314.

by a representative of the State Board of Charities and Public Welfare, Mr. Mayberry expressed the opinion that 75 per cent of the prisoners of his county could be trusted to work without guards, provided he could have half an hour's talk with each before he went out. The results show that Mr. Mayberry was conservative in his estimate. A considerably larger percentage have made good.

When visited in October by two representatives of the State Board, the force now consisting of eight men, had been loaned to the State Highway Commission, and was being used by their patrolman to improve a road in use as a detour. The regular superintendent was on a vacation. There were no guards. The patrolman in charge had no gun of any kind, as he stated in the hearing of all his prisoners. The men sleep in a camp at night; but they are not guarded, chained, or locked in. They wear no stripes or other uniform to distinguish them from other working men. They sometimes visit their families on Sunday. They report for work at seven o'clock on Monday morning. The man who has the best chance to escape, the cook, was considered a most difficult man before he was sent to the road. He had escaped once after arrest by throwing the deputy sheriff into a mill pond, and had finally been marched into jail between two officers. "You are not going to send him to the camp!" exclaimed incredulous citizens when he was sentenced to the roads. Mr. Mayberry put the matter squarely up to the man. He has not betrayed the trust.

"Vance County," the report continues, "has not gone quite so far in some respects as Alexander, . . . but she has gone far enough in the matter of discipline to make a distinct contribution to the prison history of the State." A report by the superintendent of the prison force in this county is then quoted at length. In this report the superintendent says that cleanliness is required and made possible;

that profanity and indecent language are pro-
hibited; that prisoners are given "all the privileges"
possible until they prove themselves unworthy of
such privileges; that religious services are held
every Sunday afternoon, conducted usually by the
superintendent, and attended often by the families
of the prisoners; that the aim is to teach the prisoners a "high standard of living and to return them
as better citizens to the community." [21]

Alexander County no longer maintains a camp.
Two or three other counties, however, use the
honor system. Moore has maintained a small force
under this system for several years. Whenever
they get a prisoner that the superintendent thinks
he cannot handle, such prisoner is sent to another
county where he is not worked under the honor
system.

The state has given legal sanction to reward for
good conduct as a means of discipline. The prisoner who faithfully performs the duties assigned
to him is entitled to five days per month reduction
of his sentence. [22] In those counties operating their
road systems under Article Four of the Consolidated Statutes, the county road commission may
divide the prisoners into classes according to character, and work any or all of them without guards
and without stripes. Such prisoners shall be known
as "honor prisoners," and shall be entitled to receive a reduction of at least twenty-five per cent
and not more than fifty per cent of the time they
are sentenced, for satisfactory work and good be-

[21] *Biennial Report*, North Carolina State Board of Charities and
Public Welfare, 1920-1922, pp. 86-88.
[22] *North Carolina Consolidated Statutes*, 1360.

VII. New Hanover County Prisoners Preparing Road Materials. No Stripes or Chains Are Used

VIII. A Group of Negro Prisoners Showing Stripes and Chains

havior. [23] No county, it seems, has seen fit to put this section of law into operation.

Closely connected with the problem of discipline is the problem of the prevention of escape. As has already been suggested, it is partially to prevent escapes that chains are used. It is for this purpose, too, that guards are employed. These guards are armed, usually with shot-guns. They are often, if not usually, instructed to shoot to "stop" the fleeing prisoner. Not infrequently a prisoner is killed. No distinction is made as to the offense for which the prisoner is serving the sentence. He may be a white boy serving a short sentence for stealing a ride on a train; [24] or he may be a black boy who has just finished a sentence for a misdemeanor and is being held to work out the costs in the case at a wage so low that he rightly resents the injustice. [25]

The law makes escape a misdemeanor. Formerly it was a felony. [26] Allowing an escape through negligence on the part of the officer or agent in charge is also a misdemeanor. [27] Under the ancient common law, conniving at an escape made the official an accessory after the fact in the original offense, subject to the same punishment as the offender himself. [28] Whether the readiness of guards to shoot is influenced by traditions coming down from more barbarous ages, or is due entirely to the

---

[23] *North Carolina Consolidated Statutes*, 3678.
[24] Files of State Board of Charities and Public Welfare.
[25] Files of State Board of Charities and Public Welfare.
[26] *North Carolina Consolidated Statutes*, 4404, note.
[27] *Ibid.*, 4405, note.
[28] Blackstone: *Commentaries on the Laws of England*, book IV, chapter 3, section 4; chapter 10, section 4.

the character of the men who serve as guards is a question not easily answered. "I have been here twelve months and ain't had no chance to shoot a prisoner yit," remarked a guard to one of those making this study.

This is the most serious phase of the whole problem of discipline in these prison camps. Misdemeanants, as well as more serious offenders, cannot be allowed to escape at will. Yet the shooting of a man who has been convicted of a misdemeanor and is in the act of committing another misdemeanor, for which the court can sentence him only to a short term of additional imprisonment, is to inflict the death penalty on a misdemeanant without trial, on the sole judgment of a guard, usually ignorant, often of low mentality and low moral standards. [29]

The type of supervisor and guard that may be had in most cases under present conditions, and the lack of classification of prisoners or of the facilities for classification, make the problem of discipline in the county prison road gang without resorting to inhuman methods almost insoluble.

[29] In an opinion handed down by the Supreme Court since this chapter was written, it is held that it is unlawful for an officer in charge of county convicts to shoot a misdemeanant who is attempting to escape by running away. A felon under the same circumstances may be shot. *South Eastern Reporter*, Vol. 136, No. 6, February 26, 1927, *Holloway vs. Moser*, pp. 375-79.

Under this opinion a man who has stolen $19 may not be shot for attempting to escape; but if the amount which he took happened to be $21, he may be shot for such an attempt. If, however, the guard proves a poor marksman, and the felon succeeds in his attempt to escape, the prisoner is then guilty of a misdemeanor, and, if captured and taken before the court, may be punished at most only by a short additional sentence. In actual practice recaptured prisoners in this state are not usually taken before the court. When they are, the most common sentence is thirty days; occasionally sixty days.

The problem is still further complicated by the presence of a large number of Negro prisoners. Almost any individual prison official will tell you that Negroes are more easily handled than white prisoners; but whenever one condemns flogging and other brutal methods of enforcing discipline some one is ready with the retort: "You can't handle a nigger any other way." It does not follow that prisoners cannot be worked successfully on the roads under humane methods of discipline; but it is pretty clear that such successful employment must follow the selection of a higher type of official to have charge of the prisoners and that there must be some intelligent selection of the type of prisoner who is to be assigned to work on the roads.

Chapter VII

ECONOMIC ASPECTS OF COUNTY
CONVICT ROAD WORK

DOES it pay in dollars and cents to use county convicts for road building? Ever since 1885 when Mecklenburg County "paved the way" for the practical use of convicts on the county roads, it has been assumed by the people of this state that such employment of misdemeanants and felons accomplished two purposes. First, the system worked the offender hard and long and thereby punished him; and second, it saved the county the bother and expense of hiring free laborers to build the increasingly needed highways.

Because of the apparent cheapness with which convicts are maintained, officials have been led, through a lack of adequate records, into a false sense of security in regard to the economy of convict labor, and there has been a tendency to condone and overlook lapses from the standards of high efficiency because of a feeling that the margin between the daily cost of convict and free labor was wide enough to allow a certain amount of waste. But a comparison of the costs of maintenance of convicts and wages of free labor shows that the margin of profit is narrow enough to prove convincingly the need of closer attention to detail in the employment of convicts.

It has been impossible to secure precise information regarding costs of road building by prisoners.

An entirely fair and reliable comparison can be made only where identical conditions prevail, and where adequate records are available. Estimates of the efficiency of convict labor have placed it at from 50 to 150 per cent of the efficiency of free labor. One hundred and eleven estimates from nineteen states have shown that the labor of 3,522 convicts was equivalent to the work of 3,481 free laborers, considering the same time period and that all workers possessed average skill. In the Northern states the figures indicate that 355 convicts were equal to 174 free laborers, while in the Southern states, 3,167 convicts were as good as 3,307 free men. [1]

Convict labor has been used since 1909 in Arizona on practically all types of road construction. After nine years of experience this state believes without reservation that their convict system is a source of profit. State highway officials consider that convict labor costs only two-thirds as much as the contract system. [2]

---

[1] U. S. Department of Agriculture, *Bulletin*, number 414, pp. 17-18.

[2] *American City Magazine*, (T & C ed.), February 1920, pp. 99-101.—The Arizona system comprised a central stockade; an eight-hour day; motor truck transportation. Their experience has varied from the very good and economical to the bad and wasteful. The general conclusion is that convict labor is capable of producing work of good quality, both in highway construction and in making reinforced concrete bridges, together with low costs and few escapes. It appears that such labor is more dependent on the quality of its leadership than is free labor, and that a convict camp under poor management is an annoyance and a danger, expensive and wasteful. Whenever convict labor fails to achieve beneficial results the methods and personnel of the management should be held accountable rather than the quality of the labor that is used. There are relatively few men who are gifted with the quality of leadership required in handling this class of labor. Convicts are relatively low mental types and are not good usually in handling machinery.

Convict labor on Nebraska roads was tried for the first time in 1917. Work was started in August with 37 men, a number of whom were "lifers." The road is described as 32 feet wide, curb to curb, 6" x 20" concrete curbs, 5" concrete base with a repressed brick surface, filled with asphalt placed on a sand cushion. The concrete was mixed at a central plant and hauled in regular graders' dump wagons— a satisfactory and economical method in this case. The great difficulty was the ignorance of the men, only three of whom had ever seen a paving job in process before. Only three others had ever worked at any kind of construction. It is reported that all these prisoners had great satisfaction in looking back at the end of the day to observe the work accomplished. The net saving to the state amounted to $5,624.28, using the adjoining work by a contractor as a basis of estimating the probable cost of the pavement laid by the convicts. During the ninety days of work only one prisoner, a colored boy with only four months to serve, broke parole. [3]

Considerable divergence of opinion exists regarding the comparative economic value of convict road labor and free contract road labor. Of those who express themselves on the subject a few are dogmatic, some are cautious, others are very much in doubt. Apparently political, financial, or other personal considerations have played a more prominent part in determining their attitude than a careful study of the whole problem. A type of statement frequently made and widely accepted is the following:

[3] *American City Magazine*, May 1917, pp. 483-484.

From the standpoint of economy to the State, the employment of convicts to work on the roads has advantages over any other employment. The maintenance cost is borne by the county which uses the convicts, and from the standpoint of the county, the chain gang is the cheapest means of making and keeping up good roads. [4]

The writer of the above does not take into account that convict chain gangs vary in size from half a dozen men to more than one hundred in a single camp, nor does he mention what is very important economically, namely the method of control. Many camps are bound by chains and guns, a few are controlled by the honor system. Chain gang foremen, county commissioners, and engineers, many of whom believe that convicts can construct roads at low cost, state emphatically that the ordinary chain gangs cannot maintain roads economically. The honor group may be able to do so, but honor camps of county convicts in the South are the exception rather than the rule. The great majority of county prisoners are "gun men," which means that they work under armed guards.

Much of the inefficiency of convict work results from the use of guarded convicts upon that type of road, which for its most economical construction requires a very flexible force. The construction of top-soil and sand-clay roads cannot be done satisfactorily with gang labor, but requires a force readily divided into small units. One guard can handle fifteen men. This can be done for grading, quarrying, and macadam roads, but not on cheaper roads. The experience of the Virginia Highway Commission bears out this statement.

[4] Dowd, Jerome: *The Negro in American Life*, Century, 1926, p. 144.

In Virginia where convicts were managed as well as in any state and with a lower maintenance cost than in any other state, the grading and construction of macadam roads were conducted to considerable advantage with convicts—the cost per mile was lower than with free labor. However, the average cost of sand-clay and soil roads was nearly 45% higher. These records confirm the opinion of many engineers and foremen that the use of convict labor on the light work ordinarily carried on by the counties of the southern states is a mistake. In the interest of economy it would be better were all this work done by free labor and the use of convicts confined to heavier construction and grading. But if the convicts are to be used at all on such work they should without doubt be honor men who may be organized into a fairly mobile force. [5]

The main content of the above quotations corresponds with the opinion of most of the road officials and foremen of North Carolina chain gangs, except that some of them would not concede the high cost of convict-built sand-clay or soil roads.

The use of machinery is another factor in road costs. One of North Carolina's state highway engineers makes this statement:

Neither convict nor free labor can compete with machinery. Our costs show that grading in June 1926 on Project 978 cost us $1.06½ per yard using State convict labor alone, whereas the shovel with the same crew of men brought the cost down to 48c per yard in the month of July. On project 965 B, on which we were using convict labor alone, it cost 61c whereas on Project 966 B, the adjoining project with the same material but for which we used the steam shovel and free labor, the cost was 41 c. [6]

---

[5] U. S. Department of Agriculture, *Bulletin*, number 414, pp. 23-24.
[6] Unpublished letter from Highway Engineer, October 1926.

The value of modern machinery in all kinds of heavy work is so obvious that extended discussion of this factor is unnecessary. There are, of course, conditions under which man and mule power are the only practicable methods of working. Ditching machines are not invariably useful nor is the steam shovel economical for shallow excavating. The question before the authorities concerned is whether counties shall go ahead independently using man and mule power where machinery would produce more economical and better results. As is shown elsewhere, there is far more to the county convict problem than merely "keeping convicts busy."

Since the only saving which can be made by the use of convict labor must be derived from the labor itself, it follows that the kind of work best adapted for such a system is that in which the labor itself forms the largest part of the whole cost. The Fulton County, Georgia, experimental camp has demonstrated that clearing and grubbing and certain types of excavation are best adapted for convict labor, and that such work as culvert and bridge construction is to be avoided whenever possible. [7]

With further reference to the question of construction and maintenance, some of the North Carolina county road engineers, superintendents of convict camps, officials, and contractors have given their opinions in letters and in interviews.

I consider the actual expense of doing construction work with convicts to be as great as the cost of free labor. But the convict has to be taken care of some way and if we did not work him he would cost the county

[7] *Bulletin*, number 583, U. S. Department of Agriculture, (Fulton Honor Camp, Fulton, Georgia), p. 63-64.

a considerable amount and the county would get nothing in return. Therefore, I think the best way out is to work the convict in the road camps. (Beaufort County.)

In figuring the difference between free labor and convict labor for road building, much depends on the equipment to be used, the kind of work to be done, and the number of convicts. Convict labor is more economical where the number is not too small and they do not have to be too badly scattered. They are more profitable in rough work such as clearing and grubbing and ditching. Where there are more "trusties" they are more profitable where teams are used since chained men are not economical and cannot be used with teams except in pits for loading, etc.   (Columbus County.)

For the rough work in road building we find that we can get more work for the same money from convict labor than from free labor, but for machine work and such as dragging and maintenance we find that the overhead expense makes the convict labor more costly than free. . . . We are approaching the point in our road work where for the most part it will be machine work and maintenance, and I think we will soon reach the point where convicts will not pay.
(Cumberland County.)

We estimate that the amount of road construction for the next three years will be less than in the past three years. From now on it is a question of rebuilding or renewing. Except for renewal work or new work we do not feel that convicts can be efficiently used. . . . Operating as we have been we consider the convict labor much cheaper. We conduct our camp on the honor system and even let a good many of the convicts go home on Sundays to their families. We employ no guards but have two foremen. Two or three men run off every year but there is only one that we have not caught. It costs an average of $50 apiece to catch them. The honor system as we work it has been very satisfactory from an economic standpoint.
(Moore County.)

I would not have prisoners working for me who had to do so under guard. They would be too expensive and inefficient. We are now using about sixty men from the State Prison at Raleigh. They are as good, perhaps better, than free labor for they do their utmost to give satisfactory work and dread the idea of going back to the "walls." They work a ten-hour day; get five cents per hour for themselves, and if they wish to work over-time we are allowed to give them the full 30c per hour. For the regular ten-hour day we pay the State 25c an hour for each man. The men are given considerable freedom to go and come outside of working hours, and we have had only one escape in the year.

(State Highway Contractor.)

These varying points of view very well illustrate the present lack of agreement concerning the economic value of convict labor in highway construction. The majority however, seem to emphasize the point that honor prisoners are an economic asset. Of equal importance, perhaps, is high grade management that combines business efficiency and interest in the welfare of the men. The Moore County officials state that in their four years of experience it has been necessary to change rules and regulations to suit conditions. They stress the importance of having the proper man in charge who must be neither hard-boiled and quick-tempered, nor too easy going and careless. Their camp has never been a large one, and on November 1, 1926, was made up of only six white men and twelve Negroes. In spite of the fact that this county has been operating a convict camp with fewer prisoners than the consensus of opinion would consider a minimum for economy, their figures seem to show that the direct cost per convict has been in the neighborhood of $1.00 per day only.

In October 1926 a representative group of North Carolina counties which operate convict camps, were asked to give their opinions as to (1) the lowest number of prisoners a camp should have in order for it to be a paying plan for the county, and (2) whether ordinary convicts can be used efficiently in road maintenance work with the usual number of guards. The following table has been compiled from their replies:

Counties	Convicts			Lowest number of Convicts for economy	Are ordinary, guarded convicts efficient for maintenance work?
	White	Black	Total		
Beaufort	5	15	20	20	No
Chatham	11	19	30	15	No
Columbus	13	20	33	35	No
Craven	1	26	27	20	Yes
Cumberland	8	28	36	20 to 25	No (2 camps)
Forsyth	56	107	163	30	No (3 camps)
Harnett	8	10	18	25	No
Mecklenburg	36	105	141	25	No (4 camps)
Moore	6	12	18	20 to 25	No
Rockingham	20	12	32	40	Yes
Transylvania	19	6	25	35	No
Wayne	23	67	90	30	No (3 camps)

Upon the basis of the figures given above, it would seem that the convict road camp cannot be operated economically if the number of prisoners is less than twenty-seven. It should be borne in mind, however, that where there is more than one camp in a county, great saving can be accomplished through centralized purchasing, so that a county having two camps of twenty men each is far more likely to achieve economy in either of its camps than is a county having only one camp of twenty men. Except in those counties such as Cumberland, Forsyth, Mecklenburg, and Wayne, all of which have more than one camp, the tendency as revealed in this table seems to be to set the number for economy at a point very close to or below the number of prisoners actually in camp.

These twelve counties furnish a sufficiently varied sample from several standpoints—rural and urban, geographic placement, method of convict camp operation—to produce a fair picture, fair in the sense of just. There are rural Chatham and urban Forsyth; Beaufort on the coast and Transylvania in the mountains many miles west; Rockingham in the north central and Columbus in the south; Moore with its honor system and Mecklenburg with its chains. Also this group represents all kinds and conditions of recording and accounting systems. Some seem to have no records at all worth the name; others have an accounting method meagre and of little value; and still others have good systems—Forsyth, for example. In the best systems of bookkeeping effort is invariably made to reduce to a minimum the catch-all item known variously as "sundries" or "general expense" or "miscellaneous." Among other counties whose systems of accounting bear the marks of dependability is Transylvania, this county seeming to be one of a very few which give any consideration to unit costs such as those pertaining to the moving of road materials on a cubic yard basis. Mecklenburg's elaborately computed decimals are doubtless reliable in showing expenditures for maintenance, but fail to indicate whether the county is profiting by its convict road labor.

As to the number of prisoners necessary for economy of overhead, the opinion of North Carolina officials that a convict camp of about thirty men can be operated profitably differs considerably from the conclusions of the United States Department of Agriculture:

> Whatever the work, the size of the camp should be apportioned to it. It is likely that under average conditions the number of men should be from forty to fifty. In many of the smaller counties the number of convicts on hand at one time is not more than twenty, who must be employed either inefficiently on the roads, or at some less desirable occupation, or else maintained in idleness. Under present laws in many of the states this condition must be endured, but it might be remedied by the enactment of laws placing county convicts under state control and management.[8]

A reasonable conclusion seems to be that where a camp is operated on the honor system the average number of convicts should be about twenty-five in order to effect economy, but in the ordinary chain gang where such items as pay for guards must be

---

[8] *Bulletin*, 414, p. 25.

included, the number cannot reasonably fall below thirty-five prisoners, if money is not to be wasted. [9]

In some cases where a county has so few offenders that it cannot maintain a camp of its own economically, it sends its convicts to a neighboring county when the latter chooses to pay the fines and costs for such extra road labor. Durham County, for example, receives men sentenced from five other counties. This plan approaches the nearest to the district plan, one which many people, including judges and solicitors, feel to be a good way economically to care for county convicts. A county which needed a convict camp ten years ago may not be justified in operating one today, especially when a contiguous county makes it possible for a unification of road forces and a consequent saving of money for all concerned.

Another factor in connection with economy in convict road labor is that of duration of servitude.

---

[9] Within a few miles of the University of North Carolina, there is at this writing (December 1926) a convict camp consisting of eight prisoners, a guard and superintendent. During the night hours they are housed in cages which are far from wind proof. The temperature is well below freezing. Twelve miles away and reached by good roads is Hillsboro, Orange County seat, where a $60,000 jail has recently been completed to accommodate from forty-five to fifty offenders. Since the last term of court many weeks ago, Orange County has accumulated seven persons who are quartered in this commodious jail and who await the opening of court which convenes in a few days. Whether or not the road prisoners of Orange County are being punished it is evident that the pocket books of that county's taxpayers are suffering needlessly. Why not house the road convicts in the jail and send them to work by trucks? The cost, initial and maintenance, of that camp with its tents and cages for eight men, would pay their transportation expenses to and from Hillsboro daily, and in addition there would be as a result of some such arrangement a considerable saving achieved.

The employment of short-term men is bound to result in inefficiency. In the judgment of superintendents and foremen, from thirty to sixty days are required to harden and instruct the recruit. This being so, it is obvious that road work employing misdemeanants whose terms average less than six months must bear a heavy burden of lost time and ineffective labor. This complaint was voiced by officials of Mecklenburg County and others. It is true that difficulty of this sort would more likely exist in camps which are supplied from the larger cities, where the status of offender and the type of offense vary considerably, than in the less populous regions.

As to the number of men who remain on the camp premises for cooking and cleaning, and for sickness, the total cost is only slightly affected, according to the information which has been received in this connection. In the small camp it is a factor of proportionately greater importance than in the large camp.

So long as the county authorities pay only slight attention to cost accounting, no definite conclusions can be reached concerning the economic value of convict road work. Little satisfaction exists either in trying to obtain convict camp financial records or in quoting what little can be unraveled from them. No uniformity exists among the counties in their record-keeping. They are sufficient unto themselves and the state minds its own financial business. Such figures as it has been possible to procure are not entirely convincing and cannot be used as a basis for comparing one county with another. Space and emphasis will be given only to those financial statements which seem to throw some light on the problem under discussion.

Four of the twelve counties which have submitted figures reveal for the year 1925, on a basis of 300 working days rather than 250 working days which is a more correct figure, a per capita cost per day ranging from $1.35 in a camp with 33 prisoners to $3.23 in a camp with 20 prisoners. These per capita costs are based on total camp expense. In one county it is admitted that no cost account is kept, and in two others none was submitted.

In Moore County a twelve-month prisoner working 300 days costs the county for board and tobacco, clothes, and medicine, plus his share of the recapture cost of escaped men—a total of $321.40, or about $1.07 for such a prisoner per day. This is computed from direct or personal costs only. Thirty cents per cubic yard is the estimated cost for moving dirt in this county. Sometimes in putting in fills to bridges where they have been able to use tractors with automatic load and dump wheeler, they have made the move as low as five cents per cubic yard.

The road engineer of Wayne County reports that the total cost per day per prisoner is 81½c and that mules cost 63c per day to feed—a total of $1.44½ per day per prisoner. It is not clear whether this is on the basis of 300 or 365 days. They do not have cubic yard costs but figure on the cost per mile.

Pitt County has been giving special attention to convict costs since February 1926. Of great value is the report of the county engineer which gives in some detail the cost and the approximate amount of work in the construction of ten miles of grading done in that county by its road convicts. The road was started November 1, 1925, and completed October 15, 1926. It runs through a flat swampy region consisting of a soil which is very soft and miry when wet. The work started at a point seven miles from the nearest railroad and goes ten miles in a direction away from the railroad station. Supplies, therefore, were carried from seven to seventeen miles. The amount of labor involved in this piece of road construction was as follows.

Clearing and grubbing.........	32 acres
Common excavation..........	32,522 cubic yards
Borrow excavation...........	27,481 cubic yards
Ditch excavation............	7,862 cubic yards
18″ concrete pipe in place.....	925 lineal feet
24″ concrete pipe in place.....	455 lineal feet
30″ concrete pipe in place.....	70 lineal feet
36″ concrete pipe in place.....	145 lineal feet

The total cost of the above labor amounted to $33,666. According to the estimate of the engineer the saving in doing this work by convict labor was $12,000, and he is confident that the work has been done more satisfactorily than would have been the case with contract labor.

In December, 1925, Rutherford County reëstablished a chain gang after being without one for twelve years. The following letter was received from the county official from whom information was requested:

Replying to your letter of inquiry of October 26 relative to this county establishing a chain gang, would state that it was an economic necessity. It was better for the men to work than lie up in jail. They are at least paying for their "keeping." It costs $18.00 per month for a person to stay in jail. We have better county roads since the gang was established. I have no figures to quote you on road costs and do not have time to work them up.

For fourteen months ending September 1, 1926, the convict force of Transylvania County worked on one project, moving 65,000 yards of material (unclassified) at a cost of 70 cents per cubic yard—material at least 20 per cent rock. The road was sub-graded and left in good condition for travel. There has been no account kept of breakage behind the slope stakes, which would perhaps lower the cost per yard as much as six cents. The costs above mentioned are obtained by recording the yards moved; the roads ditched, crowned, and machined ready for travel; account is taken of repairs to shovel, compressor, carts, wagons, etc.; all costs, in fact, such as pertain to salaries, guarding, and material. [10]

----

[10] Some years ago the following report was received from a North Carolina engineer working state convicts on the Hickorynut Gap Road: "I moved 522 cubic yards of what I classify as earth, though contractors would try and claim a hardpan classification for some of it. The team work cost $33.00 and I used 15 men for three days, which at $1.00 per day would be $45.00, or a total of $78.00 for moving yardage; or almost exactly 15c per yard. In fact we reduced this a little, as we hauled enough rocks for a rock culvert, and the men put it in. This would in reality bring the cost of earth excavation down to 14c per yard, some of which had to be hauled 600 feet. This is considerably better than the contractor's prices." See North Carolina Geological and Economic Survey, *Good Roads Circular*, number 97, February 18, 1914, J. H. Pratt, State Geologist.

Mecklenburg has four convict camps. The accounting system includes an adequate list of items and per capita costs figured to thousandths of a cent. For example Camp Number 1 shows for the year ending June 30, 1926, a total daily per capita cost of $2.97421, and of this amount $.76419 is charged to direct or personal cost of convict upkeep, food, clothing, guarding, medicine, etc. The chairman of the highway commission and the highway engineer give the following statement:

On high grade hard surface roads, we prefer to contract work, but on other types of construction, convict labor is cheaper we think from our records.

The highway officials of this county do not deem it necessary to measure the actual costs per unit of work accomplished and therefore it is not surprising that their opinion is in conflict with local and distant experience with convicts in building hard surface roads.

Before submitting the final illustration of local interest and the one which is perhaps the most important in this discussion, it should be emphatically pointed out that all the foregoing figures which have been submitted are not necessarily computed on the same basis, and therefore they cannot be used fairly in comparing one county with another. Their only value is that they give some clue to comparative costs between free labor at $2.50 per day and convict labor. For example, the figure for Moore County is for direct costs, whereas several others furnish total costs only. A true comparison can be made only after the closest scrutiny of many factors not revealed in the data which were available for this chapter. The requisites for measurement involve many considerations such as climatic and weather conditions, topography and type of road building, kind and extent of machine usage, methods of camp management and convict control, methods of record-keeping, and the extent to which free labor is used.

The most satisfactory and recent testimony obtainable in North Carolina is produced by Forsyth County. This information comes directly form that county's highway commission:

STATEMENT OF FORSYTH COUNTY HIGHWAY
COMMISSION
COST OF CONSTRUCTION OF STATE HIGHWAY
PROJECT NO. 740

Twelve Miles Concrete Pavement, 18 feet wide, 11″ thick at each shoulder and 7″ thick in the middle of the pavement.

Expense Camp No. 2 grading force, including pay roll of free men and guards, maintenance of prisoners, mules, and machinery repairs_____ $ 21,695.74

Expense Camp No. 5, concrete and finishing force, including pay roll of free men and guards, maintenance of prisoners and mules, machinery, repairs, side tracks, trestles_____ 58,912.73

New machinery purchased_____$33,509.38
    Less inventory value_____ 20,172.50   13,336.88

Net cost to county_____$ 93,945.35
Add prisoners' labor, 20,562 days at $2.00_____ 41,124.00
Add teams' labor, 3,380 days at $3.50_____ 11,830.00

                                                      $146,899.35
Cost of materials furnished by the State Highway Commission, sand, stone, cement, etc._____ 198,769.19
State Highway cost for engineering, etc._____ 16,575.19

                                                      $362,243.73
Contract estimate on same_____ 401,624.00

Saving or profit_____$ 39,380.27

Our records show the cost of keeping prisoners 60c per day, including food, and all camp supplies, overhead expenses, including guards, etc. Cost of mules, 60c per day.

We have kept costs of building all soil roads and find that they have run an average of $5,000.00 per mile, whereas, the State Highway Commission at the time we made this comparison, gave us a conservative figure of $7,500.00 per mile. We consider building roads by convicts an economical method and present above a full statement of our costs for approximately twelve miles of concrete road which was built under State Highway Supervision, between Winston-Salem and Greensboro. This construction shows a profit over and above all expenditures that we could count in, including a value of $2.00 per day for the convict labor, amounting to $14,124.00, which expense had already been counted in the camp expense, and the value of teams at $3.50 per day, the cost of keeping mules and prisoners already included in camp expense.

This experience of Forsyth County is worthy of special note because the prisoners were worked under guards instead of under the honor system. It is of interest to compare this report of road building in Forsyth County with the results of the Fulton County Honor Camp, Georgia, whose figures are based on the per capita and daily costs as well as on the total cost of construction.[11] This experimental camp containing on an average forty Negro convicts, was maintained for a period of ten months in 1916 on the honor system under the observation of the United States Office of Public Roads and Rural Engineering and the United States Public Health Service.

---

[11] U. S. Department of Agriculture *Bulletin*, Number 583. 1918.

COST OF CONSTRUCTION OF POWERS' FERRY
ROAD BY FULTON COUNTY HONOR CAMP [12]

Earth excavation 30,255 cubic yards, 20.6c per cubic
yard_____$ 6,236.81
Rock excavation 3,548.6 cubic yards, 54.3c per cubic
yard_____ 1,927.66
Area cleared and grubbed, 9 acres, $68.24 per acre_____ 614.17
Pipe laid, 288 linear feet, 44c per foot_____ 126.94
Masonry, 62 cubic yards, $4.83 a cubic yard_____ 299.02
Excavation for bridge, 105 cubic yards, 75c per cubic
yard_____ 72.46
Masonry, 51.6 cubic yards, $3.22 per cubic yard_____ 166.28
Gutter pavement, 4,747 square yards, 18.1c per square
yard_____ 859.40
Top-soil, 1,500 square yards, 4.7c per square yard_____ 70.07
Miscellaneous work_____ 270.00

$10,642.81

TABLE SHOWING COST OF MAINTAINING CONVICTS
AT FULTON COUNTY HONOR CAMP

Items	Cents per convict per Calendar day	Per Cent
Preparation of site_____	.0036	.7
Interest and depreciation on buildings_	.0623	12.4
Water supply_____	.0171	3.1
Sewage disposal_____	.0057	1.0
Clothing_____	.0412	7.5
Laundry_____	.0226	4.1
Furnishings and equipment_____	.0291	5.3
Kitchen and mess equipment_____	.0030	.5
Fuel and light_____	.0089	1.6
Subsistence_____	.1747	31.7
Medical_____	.0162	2.9
Transportation_____	.0475	8.7
Camp supervision_____	.1049	19.0
Tobacco_____	.0081	1.5
	.5449	100.0

[12] The length of the road constructed was 9,900 feet. The work
consisted of grading, guttering, and surfacing with top soil, together with the construction of incidental drainage structures.

Because of bad weather, Sundays and other holidays, camp duty, and sickness, the convicts actually spent only 70 per cent of their total working time on road construction. While the cost of maintenance per convict each calendar day was 54.49 cents, the actual cost of maintaining one working convict one working day, which is equivalent to the wage of labor, amounted to approximately 77 cents. It is significant that the comparatively low cost of maintenance was secured in a camp where every effort was made to provide wholesome food, adequate living quarters, and modern sanitary equipment.

It is unfortunate that the above table giving the cost of construction of the Powers' Ferry road cannot be supplemented by a contractor's bid or estimate covering the same job. The most important question to be answered is not what it costs the county to maintain its convicts, nor even the cost of building by convict labor a given piece of road, but the actual difference in cost of road construction when convict labor instead of free labor is employed. This question is not satisfactorily answered in the tables above given, nor in the remainder of the report of the Fulton County Honor Camp by the United States Department of Agriculture. Nevertheless the evidence presented in this government report does seem to justify the conclusion of the author that "The economy resulting from the employment of the convicts in this work and the high degree of efficiency with which they were maintained and organized are proved by the low unit costs of the work."

In the ten years which have intervened between the experiments in Fulton County, Georgia, and the Forsyth County road building project, considerable publicity has been given to convict road building in all parts of the country. For the most part this has pertained to state convict labor. Free men went to war and prisoners were put on the roads. Since 1920, however, very little has appeared in periodicals and bulletins regarding the system. *The American City Magazine*, which published prior to 1920 more short articles on this matter than any other single periodical, no longer gives emphasis to this subject and apparently has lost interest in the use of convict labor for highway construction. During the five-year period 1915-1919 there appeared thirty-six articles bearing directly on the subject, but in the period 1920-1924 only six substantial articles can be located.

Among the points which have been suggested in connection with the economic aspects of the county convict camp are the following:

The cheapness of convict labor may be more apparent than real.

Precise information on the question is very scarce and difficult to obtain.

Various parts of the country seem to have used both state and county convicts profitably on the roads.

There is a general feeling that roads can be constructed economically by convicts but that road maintenance by such labor in uneconomical.

Neither convict nor free labor can compete with machinery.

It is unusual to find successful convict road building ventures apart from the honor system.

The number of men in camp and their length of servitude have much to do with economy of operation.

Record-keeping has either been lacking, or inadequately done, and has no semblance of uniformity from county to county.

In conclusion, it is evident that many convict road camps in the past fifteen years have *constructed* roads economically; and that with few exceptions this has been done most successfully under the honor system. At the present time, the wider use of road machinery makes it extremely doubtful whether unskilled convicts who must be worked in a compact group under guard can any longer be profitably employed in road building. As for road maintenance, the evidence is conclusive that the chain gang is entirely unsuited for such work. From the economic point of view, it is highly essential that the counties devise some better method of segregating and correcting the able-bodied offender.

Chapter VIII

STATISTICAL STUDY OF THE CONVICT CAMP POPULATION

ON OCTOBER 1, 1926, there were approximately 2,500 prisoners in all the county chain gangs in the state. Only forty-eight of the one hundred counties at the present time maintain chain gangs, but these cover slightly more than half of the total area of the state and comprise two-thirds of the entire population. They include, moreover, nearly all of the more progressive and wealthy counties which have taken an active interest in the construction of good roads. Of the total number of prisoners on October 1, 1926, more than 1,600 were Negroes and about 800 were white. This statistical study includes 1,521 prisoners—1,036 Negroes, 469 whites, and 16 Croatan Indians. These prisoners were in thirty-three prison camps in twenty counties. [1] The study, therefore, includes about five-eighths of the county chain gang prisoners in the state. The proportion of white to Negro prisoners in the group studied is approximately the same as that for the whole state. [2]

---

[1] These counties are: Alamance, Anson, Buncombe, Chatham, Davidson, Durham, Edgecombe, Forsyth, Guilford, Johnston, Lenoir, Mecklenburg, New Hanover, Orange, Pitt, Robeson, Vance, Wake, Wilson, and the Rocky Mount Road District in Edgecombe and Nash Counties. Included in these camps were also prisoners sentenced by the courts of Alleghany, Ashe, Catawba, Cherokee, Graham, Haywood, Hertford, Jackson, Lincoln, Madison, Mitchell, Pamlico, Pender, Person, Surry, Swain, and Wilkes counties.

[2] Among the 1521 prisoners there was only one of foreign birth. He was a Greek who was serving a sentence for abandonment.

The method used in securing the information upon which this chapter is based was to go to the county and get whatever information was available from such official records as exist, to secure other information from the officials immediately in charge of the prisoners, and finally to supplement the information secured from official sources by interviewing each individual prisoner and by tests to determine his ability to read. The information thus sought included ability to read, age, occupation, residence, marital status, church membership, offense, and length of sentence. At the camp the general method of procedure was to gather the prisoners in small groups about the mess hall table, or sometimes an improvised table, and give them the educational tests. The Detroit Word Recognition Test and the Thorndike Word Knowledge Test were used. Conditions were not always the most favorable for giving the tests. Occasionally there were no tables found and the officials in charge were not inclined to assist in improvising tables. On one occasion those giving the tests had to enter a horribly filthy camp and give the tests to the prisoners and secure other information from them as they sat upon the dirty bunks to which they were chained. Usually, however, there was no lack of coöperation on the part of officials, and in less than ten cases of individual prisoners was there lack of what was apparently the fullest coöperation. Under such conditions the tests were given, and such other information as could not be obtained from official records or officials was secured from the prisoners.

The age of the prisoner was secured from official records in the two of the twenty counties involved in which such records exist. In all other cases it was secured from the prisoners. In the matter of occupation it was found necessary to rely on the word of the prisoner supplemented occasionally by that of the camp supervisor. No court in North Carolina has been found which keeps any record of the occupation of the persons convicted of offenses against the law. In the matter of residence, it was necessary again to rely on the statement of the prisoner, verified in two counties only by official record. The method here was to ask every prisoner his exact address at the time of his arrest and also the place of his birth. If these were different, and especially if they were widely separated, the prisoner was asked how long he had lived in the place he claimed as his home. On the basis of the information thus obtained, residence was classified as rural, town, or city. [3] Marital status was recorded from the statement of the prisoner, except in one county where official record of this item was found. In the attempt to ascertain what proportion of these prisoners were church members, the prisoner's statement was accepted, but no one was recorded as a church member unless able to give the name of the local church in which he claimed membership, as Rhamkatt Episcopal Church. No attempt has been made to check these statements by reference to the records of the churches named. No court records bearing

---

[3] *Town* as used in this study includes towns and villages with populations under 2,500; *city*, any place with a population of 2,500 or more.

on any of these items were found. In the few cases where certain records have been referred to as official they were records compiled by the county highway commission or the county superintendent of roads.

In the matter of offense and sentence the study was begun with the intention of accepting nothing but the official court record; but this was found so difficult to obtain as to render this course impracticable. The records of the average court in the state are kept in such a way that to find such information as is recorded concerning those convicted of crime is in itself a matter of research. In a large majority of the counties of the state there is in no office at the county seat even a list of the names of prisoners on the chain gang. The only way to find such information is to go through the journal-like docket-book. The entries here, to be intelligible, must not infrequently be interpreted by the clerk of the court. It was found expedient, therefore, to accept the records in the office of the county highway commission, or of the superintendent of the prison camp. These consisted in most cases of a file of the commitment papers. In many cases these had been allowed to accumulate for several years without removing from the file the names of the prisoners whose sentences had expired. In a few counties complete records of offense and length of sentence could not be found at the time of the visit and in the case of several prisoners from these counties, this information had to be sent to the investigators later. In one of the most populous and wealthy counties of the state there were found a dozen prisoners sent up from a recorder's court, in whose cases the official commitments did not specify the offenses for which they were sentenced to the roads. In spite of the lack of official records, however, it is believed that the following statistics are fairly accurate.

Educational Status. Many of the prisoners on the county chain gangs are practically or quite illiterate. Few have gone beyond the elementary or lower grammar grades. Very few have done any work in the high school. Twenty-nine per cent of the total number included in this study—sixteen per cent of the whites and thirty-four per cent of the Negroes—were totally illiterate. Seventy-four per cent of the whole group did not have enough education to read a newspaper. This group included fifty-two per cent of the white men and eighty-three per cent of the Negroes. Seven prisoners, all white, had finished high school or had a knowledge of the English language equivalent to that of a high school graduate. Fifteen others— twelve whites and three Negroes—were placed by the tests somewhere within the high school grades. Four received the rating of "college graduate" by the word knowledge test, and a fifth was rated as "in college." Two or three of these had actually been to college, though none was a college graduate. The others had acquired their knowledge of words without the advantage of having attended college.

Of the group of illiterates and near illiterates, two hundred and sixty-eight were boys of fourteen to twenty years of age. Of these, ten white prisoners and seventy-two Negroes were totally illiterate, and an additional group of thirty-five whites and one hundred and fifty-one Negroes were unable to read a newspaper. These groups include nine per cent of all white prisoners and twenty-one per cent of all Negro prisoners. These prisoners are within the public school ages of six to twenty-one. If the proportion holds for the whole chain gang group in the state, over four hundred twenty-five boys in the chain gangs, who are unable to read a newspaper or to qualify to vote, by age are still entitled to attend the public schools. Moreover, all these young prisoners have grown up since the state has had a compulsory school attendance law. That law, evidently, has not been enforced in the case of most of these prisoners who are normal mentally; and, if enforced in the case of those so mentally subnormal as to be unable to profit by the instruction offered in the ordinary public school, no adequate steps have been taken by the state to care for these defectives. [4]

AGE OF PRISONERS

	Under 21	21-22	23-27	28-32	33-37	38-47	48-57	58-67	Unknown	Total
	Per Cent	Per Cent	Per Cent	Per Cent	Per Cent	Per Cent	Per Cent	Per Cent	Per Cent	Per Cent
White	20	15	21	15	7.2	11.3	5.1	2.5	2.9	100
Negro	23.4	15.5	24.6	14.3	7.8	8.7	3.6	1.4	.7	100

[4] No attempt was made to determine the mental status of these prisoners. It is impracticable to attempt the necessary tests under conditions prevailing in the typical county prison camp.

Age. The prisoners range in age from fourteen to seventy years. Three hundred forty-one, or twenty-two per cent of the fifteen hundred and twenty-one prisoners were under twenty-one years of age. By race this group included twenty per cent of the white prisoners and twenty-three per cent of the Negroes. Another group comprising fifteen per cent of the whites and sixteen per cent of the Negroes were twenty-one to twenty-two years of age.

RESIDENCE OF PRISONERS

	Rural	Town	City	Total	Non-Resident
	Per Cent	Per Cent	Per Cent	Per Cent	Per Cent
White	35.2	9.4	55.4	100	16
Negro	26	9	65	100	15
Percentage Distribution General Population, 1920	71.4	9.4	19.2	100	------

Residence. Approximately sixty-two per cent of the whole number of prisoners—somewhat more than fifty-five per cent of the whites and sixty-five per cent of the Negroes—lived in towns and cities of more than two thousand five hundred inhabitants. The proportion of the total population of the state living in such towns and cities in 1920 was nineteen per cent. Twenty-eight per cent of the prisoners—thirty-five per cent of the whites, and twenty-six per cent of the Negroes—lived in the country. Of the total population in 1920, seventy-one per cent were country dwellers. Among the prisoners, approximately nine per cent of each race gave as their homes small towns with populations under twenty-five hundred. The proportion of the whole population living in such small towns, according to the last census, is also nine per cent. It was noticeable, also, that in the counties with a city of fifteen thousand population or more, crime apparently was rarely committed except in the cities; whereas in the counties without such cities the proportion for purely rural districts was greater.

Nonresidents, those who had recently come into the state, and floaters, those who by their own statements had been constantly moving from place to place and so had no fixed residence, made up sixteen per cent of the white and fifteen per cent of the Negro prisoners.

OCCUPATIONS OF PRISONERS

	Farmer	Skilled Trades	Unskilled Labor	Textile Workers	Other Factory Workers	Domestic Service	Miscellaneous	Total
	Per Cent	Per Cent	Per Cent	Per Cent	Per Cent	Per Cent	Per Cent	Per Cent
White_____	26	30.5	15	12	4	_____	12.5	100
Negro_____	22	11	47	_____	8	7	5	100

Occupation. Of the four hundred sixty-nine white prisoners, one hundred forty-three, or thirty and one-half per cent classified themselves as belonging to one or another of the skilled trades; one hundred twenty-three, or twenty-six per cent, were farmers; sixty-nine or approximately fifteen per cent, unskilled laborers; fifty-seven, or twelve per cent, textile workers; twenty, or somewhat more than four per cent, workers in other factories, mostly tobacco factories; and the remaining fifty-seven individuals, scattered among a large number of occupations. Of the one thousand and fifty-two Negroes and Croatan Indians, four hundred ninety-six, or forty-seven per cent, were unskilled laborers; two hundred thirty, or nearly twenty-two per cent, farmers; one hundred seventeen, or eleven per cent, belonged in the skilled trades—mechanics, plasterers, etc.; eighty-five, or eight per cent were workers in factories, mainly tobacco factories; seventy-five individuals were in domestic service; and the remaining forty-nine prisoners belonged to various occupations. The skilled trade group for each race is probably too large. The prisoner, eager to make the best showing for himself, whenever there was any excuse for classifying himself as a skilled rather than an unskilled laborer, probably in many cases did so. The prisoner in the presence of the census taker is apparently remarkably like other people.

Marital Status. Forty-seven per cent of the prisoners had never been married. This group included forty-four per cent of the white prisoners, and forty-nine per cent of the Negroes. Eleven per cent—twelve per cent of the white prisoners and ten per cent of the Negro prisoners—had been separated or divorced from their wives. Three per cent of the total were widowed. Thirty-nine per cent were married and were living with their families at the time of arrest.

Church Membership. Of the whole group of prisoners included in the study, thirty-eight per cent declared themselves church members. Twenty-eight per cent of the whites and forty three per cent of the Negroes were so listed. Aproximately sixty-five per cent of the general population of the state thirteen years old and over are church members. [5] The figures for males would be somewhat lower. In percentage of church membership, therefore, prisoners in the county prison camps fall considerably below the general population, but still form a large part of the chain gang group. The church is paying little attention to this group of its erring members. In only one of the group of counties included in this study was anything approaching regular religious services reported. Usually such services are held only at infrequent intervals. No religious denomination in the state has any organized program for the reclamation of these men and boys.

MORE FREQUENT TYPES OF CRIME
Percentage of Totals for Each Race

	Crimes of Violence	Larceny	Breaking and Entering	Forgery and Check-flashing	Offenses against Morality	Violation of Prohibition Law
	Per Cent	Per Cent	Per Cent	Per Cent	Per Cent	Per Cent
White_____	13	25	4	5	5	39
Negro_____	16	31	8	3	3	24

Offenses. Offenses for which men are sentenced to hard labor on the roads range from inability to pay fine or costs, "hoboing," and "failure to pay

[5] This statement is based on the 1916 U. S. Census, the latest figures available.

auto hire" to murder. In this study violation of the prohibition laws heads the list for white prisoners with one hundred sixty cases out of a total of four hundred sixty-nine, or thirty-nine per cent of the whole. Larceny follows with one hundred eighteen cases, or twenty-five per cent. Affrays and assaults, with forty-nine cases, make up another ten per cent, while all crimes of violence amount to thirteen per cent of the total. Among the Negroes larceny appears most frequently. Three hundred twenty-eight, or thirty-one per cent of the total, were charged with this offense. Two hundred forty-eight, or twenty-four per cent, had been convicted of violation of the prohibition laws; and one hundred forty-two, or thirteen and one-half per cent, of affrays and assaults, while all crimes of violence made up sixteen per cent of the crimes charged against Negroes.

An attempt was made to find whether there was any correlation between the type of crime and the various other items included in the study. The Negro offender appears more liable to commit crimes of violence. John Charles McNeill in one of his poems makes a Negro who is describing a free-for-all fight, say,

"En I seed one fool er-fightin' wid his han's."

The Negro does not get sentenced to the roads for fighting with his hands any more frequently than the white man, but assaults with a "deadly weapon" form a larger percentage of his offenses, and he is more frequently convicted of violence against women. House-breaking, including all breaking and entering, constitutes eight per cent of his crimes;

and larceny thirty-one per cent. The white prisoner's record in these two offenses is four per cent and twenty-five per cent, respectively. The white man, on the other hand, appears more prone to forgery and check flashing, to offenses against morality, and to violation of the prohibition law.

LENGTH OF SENTENCE

	3 Mos. or Less	4-5 Mos.	6-11 Mos.	12-17 Mos.	18-23 Mos.	2 Yrs. to 35 Mos.	3 Yrs. to 47 Mos.	4 Yrs. to 59 Mos.	5 Yrs. to 9 Yrs., 11 Mos.	10 Yrs. and Over	Total
	Per Cent	Per Cent	Per Cent	Per Cent	Per Cent	Per Cent	Per Cent	Per Cent	Per Cent	Per Cent	Per Cent
White	10	13	28	23	10	11.4	3	.6	1	----	100
Negro	15.4	11	24	19	8	12	5	2.1	3.1	.4	100

Sentences. Sentences to the roads range from fifteen days, imposed by recorders' and justices of the peace courts in cases such as trespass and being drunk and disorderly, to ten years, occasionally imposed, usually in the case of a prisoner against whom there are charged several crimes, or several technical offenses involved in a single crime. The largest single group involved in this study, thirty-eight per cent of the total, were serving from one to two years. Seven per cent of the white prisoners and ten per cent of the Negroes were serving sentences shorter than three months. On the other hand, six per cent of the white prisoners and eleven per cent of the Negroes were serving sentences of three years or more. This difference in the sentences of the races is quite interesting. The larger percentage of short sentences imposed on Negroes as compared with whites probably means that there is a larger percentage of Negroes who are unable to pay a small fine or costs in case of petty offenses. On the other hand, the fact that the chances of receiving a sentence to the roads of three years or longer are two to one against the Negro as compared with the white man suggests that justice is not blind to the color of a man's skin. This apparent discrimination against the Negro may take a different form from that suggested here: it may be that certain of the more serious offenders among the whites are sent to the state prison, when a Negro charged with the same offense would be sentenced to the roads, because a sentence to the state prison is considered less humilating than one to the chain gang. Further studies of the entire prison population of the state must be made before accurate statements concerning this apparent discrimination against the Negro offender can be made.

Studied in relation to types of crime, this difference in length of sentence shows interesting variations. In all cases of offense involving violence against the person the ratio of sentences of three years or longer is 10.3 to 7.5 in favor of the white man. In the case of the one item of assault on women, including those attacks officially designated as "assault with intent to commit rape" and "assault on a female," the Negro draws the much heavier sentence. Here it is hardly necessary to suggest that these are usually cases of attacks by

Negroes on women of their own race. Yet nearly one-fourth (24.4 per cent) of the Negroes charged with this offense were serving sentences of three years or longer, while no white man was serving a sentence for the same offense as long as three years. On the other hand, sixteen and two-thirds per cent of the whites charged with such assaults were serving sentences shorter than three months. Only six per cent of the Negroes so charged were serving such short sentences. Questions as to the value of the figures on this item are raised, however, by the small number of prisoners serving sentence for assault on women—six white men and thirty-three Negroes.

The Negro bootlegger pays more dearly than the white bootlegger. The chances of drawing a sentence shorter than three months, it appears from our chain gang group, is eight to five in favor of the white man. The probabilities of a sentence of three years or longer are practically two to one against the Negro.

In punishments for offenses against morality, on the other hand, the Negro is given the advantage over the white man. The more common offenses under this head are bigamy, fornication and adultery, and prostitution. In sixteen per cent of such cases white offenders were serving sentences of three years or longer, while only three per cent of the Negroes were serving sentences of the same length. On the other hand, twenty-two per cent of the Negro offenders against morality were serving sentences under three months and twelve and one-half per cent of three to five months. No white men in this group were serving sentences under three months and only seven per cent, sentences of three to five months. For the single offense of fornication and adultery, no whites were serving under three months; five per cent, three to five months; thirty-three per cent, six to eleven months; fifty-three per cent, one to two years; and nine per cent, three years or longer. Of the Negroes, thirty-nine per cent were in for under three months; twenty-two per cent, for three to five months; twenty-two per cent, for six to eleven months; seventeen per cent, for one to two years; and none for three years or over. For prostitution considered alone, however, there is a different record. Of the Negro prisoners, two-thirds were serving sentences of one to two years, and one-third, of from six to eleven months. Of the white prisoners, two-thirds, also, were serving terms of from one to two years; but only one-sixth were in the next group, serving from six to eleven months, and one-sixth were in for three to five months. Here the race complex is probably at work. The Negro is not infrequently the solicitor for the white woman.

In the study of age in relation to type of crime, two things stand out. The first is the number of very young offenders who are sent to the roads for larceny and breaking and entering. Those charged with these allied offenses who were not over seventeen years old constituted nine per cent of all the Negroes serving sentence for this type of offense and fifteen per cent of the whites. The second outstanding fact is that violators of the prohibition law are largely older men. Of the white prisoners for all offenses thirty-five per cent were under twenty-three years old; fifty-four per cent were under twenty-seven; and forty-six per cent over twenty-seven. Of the liquor men twenty-eight per cent were under twenty-three; forty-nine per cent, under twenty-seven; and fifty-one per cent over twenty-seven, a difference of six per cent in this last group. Of the Negroes as a whole, thirty-four per cent were under twenty-three; sixty-three per cent under twenty-seven; and thirty-seven per cent over twenty-seven. Of the Negro liquor law violators, only ten per cent were under twenty-three; thirty-nine per cent were under twenty-seven; and sixty-one per cent were over twenty-seven. For both races the number of violators of the prohibition law in each age group continues large until after the age of forty-five. In most offenses it falls off very rapidly after the age of thirty.

From the point of view of occupation, among the white prisoners, fifty-seven per cent of the crimes for which farmers had been sent to the roads were violations of the prohibition law. Next to violations of the Turlington Act came larceny with eighteen per cent of all offenses by the white farm group. White prisoners who placed themselves in the various occupations included under the general term "skilled trades" proved more inclined to commit offenses against property. Larceny constituted one-third of the offenses committed by this group. Violation of the liquor law followed with twenty-two per cent. Textile workers, on the other hand, so far as this study shows, seldom violate the liquor laws. Larceny is their most frequent offense. Twenty-eight per cent of such workers on the roads were convicted of this crime. The unskilled laborer ranks next to the farmer as a violator of the prohibition law. Forty-three per cent of such white laborers on the county chain gangs were sent up for this offense. An additional thirty per cent were serving terms for larceny. Among the Negro prisoners, the largest group of farmers, forty-four per cent, were serving sentences for violation of the prohibition law. The second largest group, including twenty per cent of the total, were charged with larceny. Of the skilled trade group, thirty-five per cent were convicted of larceny, and twenty-seven per cent of violating the liquor laws. Of the unskilled Negro laborers thirty-three per cent were in for larceny and thirteen per cent for violation of the liquor laws. Of the minor offenses from the point of view of frequency of occurrence, the most important is the group of crimes of violence. In these offenses, mainly assaults of varying degrees of seriousness, the Negro laborer leads with seventeen per cent of the offenses charged to that group. Then follow the white textile worker and the Negro farmer, each with fourteen per cent; and the white farmer and the Negro skilled laborer, each with eleven per cent.

A consideration of types of crimes from the point of view of the residence of the offender involves some duplication, since the countryman is usually a farmer. Country dwellers constituted thirty-five per cent of the white prisoners. This thirty-five per cent were charged with fifty-four per cent of the violations of the prohibition law and forty-five per cent of the crimes of violence committed by the white group. Small town dwellers constituted nine per cent of the white prisoners. They exceeded their quota of crime in larceny, breaking and entering, and offenses against morals. The city group, including fifty-five per cent of the white prisoners, were charged with eighty-three per cent of the forgery and check-flashing, sixty-one per cent of the larceny, and seventy-four per cent of the abandonment and non-support, charged against the whites. Negro rural dwellers constituting twenty-six per cent of the Negro prisoners, were charged with forty-three per cent of the violations against the prohibition law committed by their race, fifty-six per cent of the abandonment and non-support, and thirty-seven and one-half per cent of the cases of carrying concealed weapons. Negro small town dwellers exceeded their quota of nine per cent, in carrying concealed weapons, abandonment and non-support, offenses against morals, and crimes of violence. Negroes living in cities furnished sixty-five per cent of the Negro chain gang prisoners. This group furnished seventy-six per cent of such prisoners of that race charged with house-breaking and other breaking and entering, seventy-one per cent of those charged with forgery and check-flashing, seventy-four per cent of those convicted of larceny, and seventy per cent of the offenders against morals.

If the chain gang group may be taken as an index, white married men commit acts of violence more often than single men. Married men are the chief violators of the prohibition law for both the white and the Negro race. Single men of both races commit more than their quota of larceny and its allied offense, breaking and entering, and of offenses against morals.

Chapter IX

CASE HISTORIES OF TYPICAL NEGRO CONVICTS

IN ORDER to supplement the statistical description of the convict camp population given in the preceding chapter, there are here presented several life histories of Negro convicts who may be regarded as fairly representative of the men of that race sentenced to county chain gangs. The collection of this material has proven to be a laborious and somewhat disappointing task because of the small amount of data available in the records of both official and private agencies dealing with the problem of crime. In the cases studied, the existing written material consisted largely of meager court and police records and the brief statements of the physical examination by the county physician. The other facts for the most part had to be collected through personal interviews with the prisoner himself, his relatives, friends, employers, county officials, and others who had some knowledge of his career. This has required in a rural state like North Carolina a great amount of time and expense in travel. The problem has been still further complicated in the case of the Negro convicts by difficulty in securing reliable family histories from people of low social and economic status, who may be both ignorant and also suspicious of the investigator. These handicaps have made it impossible to prepare the usual type of case study based on the records of well-equipped social and health agencies with which the criminal and his family have come in contact.

Nevertheless, in spite of these limitations, it is believed that these records of criminal careers of men serving time on the roads are of real interest and value to students of the perplexing problems of crime and punishment. Every possible effort has been made to present a true picture of the men studied. Special care was taken in the verification of the statements of the convicts, and where this was not possible, it is so indicated in the record. On the whole these case histories may be accepted as typical pictures of chain gang habitues, men who are perhaps the inevitable wreckage of our social and economic system. Even though these records are too inadequate to throw much light on the causation of crime, their justification may be found in the convincing evidence they present of the futility of the chain gang system under existing methods of administration.

LIFE HISTORY OF TOM SIMPSON [1]

Tom Simpson, in 1909, at the age of sixteen, left his small home town, Alston, North Carolina, and after spending one month in Barnsville, North Carolina, went to the still larger city of Carlton, North Carolina. It will be noted that his criminal career began within a year after he reached Carlton. Although he grew up in an exceptionally good home, he became restless at the age of sixteen and the resulting stricter supervision by his parents

---

[1] Assumed names of individuals and North Carolina Communities are used in the case histories given in this chapter.

merely aggravated the dicontent which they tried to remove. His religious background plays an important part in his life story. He lives in a world of spirits. He believes he is the victim of a hoodoo doctor, but he plans to out-hoodoo the hoodoo by taking the Lord as his champion. He has always taken an active part in church work. Before leaving home, he was church organist. When he reached Carlton, he at once lined up with a local church and always, when off the roads, attended church regularly and not infrequently teaches a Sunday School class. None of Tom's sisters, nor his father nor his mother, has ever been arrested.

Criminal Record

Date	Charge	Judgment
1910	Carrying concealed weapon	$5.00 fine and costs
1911	Larceny	Appeal
1913	Assault	$5.00 fine and costs
1918	Robbed Negro, with gun	Settled out of court
1921	Robbed white man, with gun	2 years on roads
1923	Forgery	2 years on roads (2 charges)
1925	Reckless driving	$5.00 fine
1925	Robbed white man, with gun	2 years on roads

General Characteristics

Tom is typically Negroid, with short kinky hair, thick lips, wide, flat nose, and rough black skin. He has an impediment of speech and talks with his hands while stammering; what he lacks in facility of speech he makes up by gestures. When he is excited, it seems that he has to exert special effort to make a statement; when calm, he talks rather easily. He has a very high affectivity score, responding very quickly to various stimuli. He is a typical "white man's nigger," very obliging, especially to his superiors about the convict camp, and seems to be consciously doing and saying that which will please them.

Physical Condition

In July 1926 the county physician reported the following facts concerning his physical condition: age, 33 years; weight, 155 pounds; height, 5 feet, 10 inches; blood pressure, systolic 160, diastolic 100; heart rate 80-90, no murmurs present; skin, eyes, nose, ears, throat, and limbs normal; teeth in bad condition; nervous; Wassermann reaction four plus.

Mental Status

Tom posed as a Shaw University student, but when given the Thorndike word test he scored only sufficient points to make the sixth grade. Later a mental examination made by a psychologist showed that he had a mental age of 11 years, four months, and an I.Q. of 71.

Tom is the only boy and the youngest of seven children. His six sisters live at various places throughout the United States—Jackson, Baltimore, Md., Pittsburg, Pa., Carlton, and Alston.

Tom's father, Charles Simpson, was sixteen years of age when the Emancipation Proclamation became effective. As a slave, he was owned by Judge Simpson and, in spite of slavery, had two whole brothers, but had no half brothers or sisters by his mother. Hariette Hicks Simpson, Tom's mother, was one of the slaves belonging to the Hicks family. The Simpson and Hicks plantations were near the little town of Alston.

Both of Tom's parents are now (1926) over seventy-five years of age. They are very highly respected by both whites and Negroes in the county and town where they have always lived. They take great pride in speaking of their early life. When Charles was set free, his master seems to have given him nothing but a name—he received no mule and land, as he had hoped he would. Hariette also took the name of her master's family. She, upon emancipation, was employed as nurse by one of her ex-master's daughters, and was so much respected by this prominent family that she was given a mahogany set of furniture for staying with them until she married. She was almost like one of the family and when Charles proposed to her he had to get the permission of her "missus." Even yet, the children whom she nursed respect her and not infrequently leave their busy offices to pay a visit to their "Aunt Hariette." Charles is one of the traditional lawn fixers in the town of Alston and still works, although he is so old and bent that he can work but half a day at a time.

Tom at Home with His Parents

When Charles and Hariette married, they bought a few acres of land near the Simpson plantation. They lived at this place until a fire burned everything they had. The family then moved to Alston and has remained there since. Tom, who was ten years old when they moved to town, began going to school regularly for the first time in his life; prior to this time he had gone only part of the time—when the roads were not too bad and he was not needed at home.

Tom got along fairly well in school, except for an impediment of speech. He stated that as a child he stammered and stuttered so badly that it was embarrassing for him to attend school. Nevertheless he continued until the age of sixteen, when he had finished, as he claimed, the sixth grade. Even before Tom quit school he had become quite famous in his home town as a pianist, and not infrequently played at the "white folks' parties."

Off to the City

Many of Tom's friends, who had gone to Carlton, kept begging him to join them. In the meantime, his parents had not allowed him to drink, smoke, or "have a good time." This supervised life became boring to him, and, in spite of the fact that he was the church organist, he became more restless each month. His pals were leaving the old home town, and he wanted to roam, too. Consequently, as his parents tightened down on him, he became more restless and irresponsible in his actions. Finally at the age of 16 he broke away from his parents and left home for the city.

In the City

In 1909, after spending a month at Barnsville, Tom went to the city of Carlton. For the first five years he worked with the Carlton Municipal Hospital and was so well liked by the authorities at the hospital that of all Negroes he was most frequently called on for special errands. His manners were good, he could see what to do, and he knew how to do things. After finishing his day's work at the hospital, he caroused, roamed, and smoked. The city, with its large Negro population, gave him abundant opportunity to live the wild life which had been impossible while under the control of his parents.

When Tom was twenty-two years of age (1915), he married. About this time he quit working at the hospital and began driving a truck for a local coal and ice company. He was an efficient worker and in addition to his routine labors he kept the trucks in repair. He worked seven years with this company. The owner stated that Tom was the best Negro worker he had ever had in his employ and, further, that he was an exceptional mechanic, keeping all twenty of the trucks in good condition.

Tom was liked by his fellow truck drivers. His sputtering and stammering amused them, and, moreover, what is more to the point, because of his ability as a mechanic he could get many concessions from the manager for the entire group of truck drivers. One evening, however, Tom scared his fellow workers when he, while partially drunk, held up one of the drivers at the point of a pistol and took his money. The man who was robbed called the manager. Tom pretended that he was innocent and agreed to give up his gun and the money only after he had been taken by the manager within a stone's throw of the city jail for the third time: the first time he handed the money over, the second time he gave up his gun, the third time he agreed to shake hands with the fellow whom he had robbed. The manager stated that he would have taken this into court had Tom been a less valuable part of his working force.

Tom's Crimes, Trials, and Judgments

Within three years of this incident (1918), Tom, disguised with a red handkerchief over his face, entered the store of J. P. Hammer and at the point of his Colt automatic, forced him to hand over all the money he had in the safe. Since Mr. Hammer suspected Tom of the crime, he directed the officers to Tom's house and within a few minutes the roll of bills and the gun described were located. Tom was taken to jail. He pleaded his own case and was sentenced to the county roads for a period of two years.

Tom's neighbors stated that he had been living a "high life" about that time: that he had bought a Victrola for one woman, a silk dress for another, and various costly things for still others. While he was flirting with these women, his own wife was off with other men. In the meantime, Tom had bargained with his employer for an old Cadillac. He and some of his buddies rode in great style after work hours, but as Tom got on the chain gang before he had made the first payment, the car automatically reverted to his former employer. It is the expressed opinion of Tom's church friends that he was living beyond his means and so was driven to robbery in order to procure the money he needed. When Tom went to the roads, he posed as a Shaw University student and, as a result, the superintendent of the camp used him to do special tasks and not infrequently had him copy orders and do other quasi-stenographic work. Being a good prisoner, he was made a "trustee" and was given his "good time." He left the roads, telling the superintendent that he had done the best he could while at camp, and that he was never coming back.

The manager of the coal and ice company was glad to get Tom back into his employ. Within eight months, however, he was in jail again. It seems that his funds ran low again, and this time he replenished them by forging checks. He got by with one, but was apprehended while waiting for the amount of the second. At his trial he was sentenced to the county roads for two years. As the first time, he was accepted as a Shaw University student, was a "trustee," and at the end of two years, less "good time," he was off.

During Tom's first stay on the roads his wife, when charged with prostitution, claimed that she would live with him when he came back, but she didn't, although it was Tom's expressed desire, and when he got on the roads the second time she left him permanently. At present (1926), he does not know where she is.

When Tom had finished his second sentence, he as usual took a very active part in church work. He told the whole congregation that he was done with "sin," that he had served the devil long enough. No sooner was he off the roads than he began working for a local contractor, driving a sand truck. In spite of his good intentions he was again on the county roads within eight months. This

11

time he stole the truck which he had been driving during the day, put on a part of a load of cement, and drove through the city of Carlton at night on his way to the store west of Carlton where the convict camp had been located while he was serving his second sentence. Before reaching the store, he threw the cement into an old barn. The store was closed. Tom met the storekeeper going to his home; he leveled a pistol at him and demanded his money. The robbed man called the officers from Carlton and within an hour Tom was overtaken and the money found by the side of the road. He was placed in jail.

Some of Tom's friends went to see him in the city jail, but he refused to talk. Many of his best friends thought that he was mentally unbalanced. He refused to retain a lawyer or to allow any one else to retain one. When the trial came, Tom told the Judge that he was guilty, that he was sorry for his "sins," and that he was anxious to pay in full for all he had done. He even begged the judge to permit him to pay in full. It seems that the Solicitor after presenting the State's evidence recommended to the judge that Tom be given a light sentence, since he had proven that he was sincere by "telling the truth" and not asking for a light sentence. Tom repeatedly told the Judge that he was through with "sin." The sentence of the court was two years on the county roads for holding up a man on the public highway and robbing him, with an additional two-year suspended sentence for the theft of the cement and truck. Back to the county roads went the "Shaw University student"; again he was made a "trustee," and is now (1926) serving his sentence as a model prisoner.

The "Shaw University Lie"

When questioned in detail about Shaw University, Tom could give no satisfactory answer as to the time that he spent there, the books he studied, the names of his professors, the names of the buildings, or the names of the students. As Tom was further questioned about his alma mater, he became quite ill at ease. Finally, he took care to see that neither the road superintendent nor any of his fellow prisoners were in hearing distance. He then explained with great satisfaction that he was no Shaw University student at all, and that he had told the "Shaw lie" as a means of getting along. Amid much stammering he said: "Ef youse come out here as a 'nordinary nigger, neber been nowhare, never seed nothin', don't know nothin'—well, youse fares putty bad—so, youse see, dat Shaw business is des a Shaw lie, and I des tole dat 'Shaw lie' to he' myse'f."

Tom's Fight with the Devil

Tom had been a very active member of the local Baptist Church, having been leader of prayer meeting, choir director, chairman of the board of ushers, and so on. He played the piano when off the roads the first time and again the second time. He painted signs for revival services, one of which is as follows: "FOR THE NEXT WEEK WE WILL WEDGE WAR AGAINST SIN." The sexton stated that Tom was one of their very best workers, but that they could not keep him off the roads. Tom's mother-in-law is a member of the same church; she is thoroughly convinced that he is in the power of the devil. She looks upon him as a puppet which does bad only because of the manipulating antics of the devil. Tom, himself, is continually repeating that he is done with the devil, and that he has taken the Lord on his side.

The fact that he was the agent of the devil was stressed in the trial. According to his own statements, he was in the hands of the devil each time that he got on the roads. The devil was put into him by a hoodoo doctor, who was hired by a man who wanted his wife. Tom does not consider himself responsible for his actions; it is the devil which the hoodoo doctor put into him that makes him do these things. Tom goes so far as to say that he "falls" at certain regular intervals due to the phases of the moon.

He is certain that he has found a means of out-hoodooing the hoodoo, for the Lord, at his call, will chase the devil out of his life for all time. He speaks of all this as though a great conflict were going to occur at some place quite apart from himself. He visualizes how the devil will be contentedly gloating over his victim, when of a flash the Lord will appear. The devil will be surprised, but will regain his wits and go to the fight instantly. Tom plans to stand off and see the Lord—his champion—crush and kill the devil. Thus he plans deliverance from this power which keeps sending him to the roads.

Conclusions

It will be noted that Tom fell into anti-social behavior as soon as he reached the city and that he went to the city so as to have a good time and be free from his parents' watchful supervision. He was an efficient worker, having been with the hospital for five years and with the ice and coal company for many years. It seems that he wanted to live a faster life, however, than his income would permit—drive a Cadillac, present women friends with expensive gifts—and so he resorted to forging checks and robbing people to effect his ends. Doubtless his mind, and body as well, are deteriorating under his chronic syphilitic condition, and this perhaps accounts in part for the lack of plans in his robberies, as well as the objective significance he attaches to spirits. But, in spite of the fact that he had a Wassermann reaction of four plus and was diagnosed as feeble-minded, he nevertheless understood to a remarkable degree just how to make the best of situations.

In speaking of the "Shaw lie," Tom said that he had just used the best means that he could find in getting along in the convict camp. Then in his stammering way he said: "I am no fool; yes, I am a fool, too!" He told a lie to get along on the roads; he succeeded. But at the same time he had only lightened his lot, which was due to a hoodoo doctor. "I am no fool; yes, I am a fool, too!" is a very fitting descriptive phrase for the superstitious existence of Tom Simpson—a "Shaw University student" now on the roads for the third time.

Ham Taylor stated that he was born on a rented farm near Martin, North Carolina. When he was three years of age, his mother died, and he and two younger brothers and both sisters were taken to Martin, where they were placed with kinsfolk. His oldest brother remained with his father. Ham pretended to be going to school regularly from the time he was seven until he was twelve, but, as a matter of fact, he attended only about one month in all. When only twelve years of age, he began to sell cocaine and the same year left Martin, going first to Cincinnati, Ohio; then to Polk, N. C.; Cleveland, Ohio; Chicago; Philadelphia; West Virginia; Richmond, Virginia; Memphis, Tennessee; Martin; France; New York City; and then back to Polk, where he has remained since 1920. In connection with his "dope" business, he stated that he attached himself to some woman who would keep his business going while he was away on pleasure trips and otherwise. The woman's house, where he lived in Polk, is located in one of the cheapest Negro districts there and she is notorious because of her house. Recently her rooms have been searched twice by federal officers looking for cocaine. It will be noted below that he has been before the courts in Polk since 1919, having had nineteen charges brought against him—larceny

[2] It was not possible to verify Ham's story in every detail, for none of his brothers or sisters was located and he has lived an anonymous life in so far as possible. Although he has lived an impersonal unattached life, moving from place to place as he sold dope and stole for a livelihood, parts of his story have been verified and substantiated in detail, while other parts, which seem quite impossible, are mentioned merely for what they are worth.

leading with seven, all of which occurred within the
ten months before he got on the roads the last time,
gambling two, assault with deadly weapon two, and
one, each, of fornication and adultery, attempt to
rape, assault, resisting an officer, violating health
ordinance, vagrancy, and reckless driving. Although he claimed that he had never been arrested
except in Polk, he doubtless has records in other
cities. These could not be obtained, however, since
he went by other names when away from Polk.
Therefore, his court record is limited to that which
was procured from Polk.

Court Record

Date	Offense	Judgment
12- 6- 9	Assault with deadly weapon	$5.00 and costs
7-31-11	Fornication and adultery	4 months
7-31-11	Assault with deadly weapon	30 days
7-31-11	Resisting officer	30 days
9-18-13	Attempt to rape	Nolle pros with leave
6-28-15	Assault	Judgment suspended
1-30-20	Vagrancy	Nolle pros
2- 9-20	Gambling	Costs
3-30-20	Health ordinance	Costs
9-11-22	Reckless driving	
2-16-23	Larceny	$25.00 and costs
2-33-23	Larceny	2 years suspended sentences
10- 8-23	Gambling	$5.00 and costs
12-10-23	Larceny	6 months
12-10-23	Larceny	6 months
12-10-23	Larceny	6 months
12-10-23	Larceny	6 months
12-10-23	Larceny	6 months

General Characteristics

Ham Taylor has smooth, black skin, which appears to be very dry and paper-like, short, kinky

hair, small, piercing eyes, broad, wrinkled fore-head, high cheek bones, and a narrow, pointed chin. He moves his head very quickly, almost by jerks, and also shows other signs of extreme nervousness in his posture, continually swinging his feet, gnawing his fingers, etc. As he talks, he not infrequently asserts that he is telling the truth, although not questioned. He considers himself quite success-ful and takes pride in asserting that he is among the few who can afford to patronize the most ex-pensive gambling houses throughout the country. He found it rather hard to get accustomed to the pick and shovel, but now that he is on the roads he takes it as a matter of course.

Physical Condition

Age, twenty-nine years; weight, 150 pounds; height, 5 feet, 9 inches; blood pressure, systolic 125, diastolic 90; heart beat 72, no murmurs pres-ent; skin, nose, and ears normal; eyes poor; throat and teeth normal; appetite irregular; Wassermann reaction, four plus.

Mental Status

Upon examination, it was found that Ham Tay-lor had a mental age of seven years, six months, and an I. Q. of 47. He was also entirely illiterate.

Parentage and Early Life

According to Ham's story he was born in 1897 on a rented farm near Martin. When he was three years old, his mother died, and seven years later his father died. At the time of his mother's death, he was sent to live with an aunt in Martin, while two of his younger brothers and both sisters were also placed with kinsfolk. His oldest brother stayed on the rented farm with his father. Ham stated that his aunt tried to make something of him, but he willingly and voluntarily affirmed that she had failed miserably. In his characteristic way, he went on to say that for five years she fixed lunches for him, but instead of going to school he went up town, picked up bottles, shined shoes, and bought rags for a rag man. He had nothing to do at his aunt's home, and as soon as he got started making money he began to stay away for a few days at a time. By the time he was twelve years of age, he left his aunt's home, but before leaving Martin, he found work in the home of a wealthy white family. At this time he had already become addicted to sniffing cocaine and drinking liquor. He procured the cocaine from a Negro dope peddler and the liquor from the white people for whom he worked. With the assistance of others he gradually entered the business of selling dope and made money. With money made from selling cocaine, and living a night-life far in advance of his years, he soon began to roam. In the meantime, he had learned much about the technique involved in the "snow" business. Martin was too small a place for this unattached young Negro with money, so he went to Cincinnati, Ohio, and after a six-months' stay there journeyed back to Polk, where there were many more Negroes than in Martin. His sales, however, had not been limited to Negroes in Martin, for he sold to whites as well.

Ham in Business

No sooner had Ham arrived in Polk than he attached himself to a "snow" agent. He made a living at this kind of business, supplemented by his occasional larcenies. When he arrived at the convict camp, in December, 1923, he stated that he had never done any work since he left the shoe shine parlor in Martin some sixteen years earlier.

He tells an interesting but unverified story of the way he conducts his illicit dealing in drugs. He began by selling "snow" on commission when he was twelve years of age. Later he bought the amount he could sell, paying cash for it, and putting the profit in his pockets. As time went on, he learned the sources of supply and how to obtain it, so by the time he had been in Polk five years he had a "snow" business of his own.

He now buys it by $140.00 lots. It is smuggled into Polk from Virginia. The technique involved is something like this, so he says: Some fellow puts two $70.00 jars into a new suit case and boards the train for Polk. Ham, or one of his agents, also with a new suit case, gets on the train and meets him at some station on the way. They know each other when they meet and merely "accidentally" swap suit cases. When the other fellow's suit case gets back to Polk, another $140.00 batch of cocaine is on hand, ready for distribution.

Ham then goes to a local druggist and buys a large number of small quinine bottles, which cost twenty-five cents each. The quinine is poured into the sink and the bottles are filled with "snow," "happy dust," or "coke," as the prospective consumer designates. The $70.00 jars of cocaine retail for $400.00. Ham stated that he had plenty of agents; for, according to him, any fellow selling 'coke' can do some business. Dope fiends never limit themselves to one specific agent.

Ham stated that he had made a great deal of money, but had spent most of it as he went, living a high life in Polk and elsewhere.

For the past six years Ham has been operating a "snow" business regularly in Polk. When he goes off he has the woman with whom he has been living send him money as he telegraphs for it and also keep a supply of "coke" for his agents to sell.

Ham's Woman

He stated that he had always lived with some woman who would take care of his business for him when he was away. He willingly gave the name and address of the woman with whom he was living when he got on the roads in 1923. Upon investigation she was located in an apartment over a vacant store in an unpainted, dilapidated, barn-like building in one of the cheapest Negro districts of Polk. She has these rooms for rent. Her place has a bad reputation—dope, liquor, and lewd women, according to reports, seem to abound. At one time she was married, but she stated that she had been "rid" of a man for several years, having "divorced" him. It was learned from her neighbors that, since Ham had been on the roads, her rooms have been raided several times by federal officers searching for cocaine. They found liquor, but no cocaine was located.

His Travels

Ham stated that, in addition to his pleasure trips, he had been in several states. According to his story he left Martin in 1909 and spent six months in Cincinnati, Ohio. Then, in the winter of 1909 he arrived at Polk, where he stayed until 1915. From Polk he went to Cleveland, Ohio, for four months (1915), Chicago for one and one-half years (1916), Philadelphia for one month, West Virginia eight months (1917). Then, after a short stay in Richmond, Virginia, and Memphis, Tennessee, he returned to Martin (1917) just before going to France, where he stayed one and one-half years (1919). When he returned from France, he spent six months in New York. He got back to Polk before Christmas, 1919. Except for pleasure trips, he stated that he had been in Polk since that time. It will be noted that this story of his in no way conflicts with his court record in Polk.

Ham Taylor—"Stall Boy"

Ham uses cocaine, drinks liquor regularly, has no insurance, belongs to no church in Polk: "Well, you see, it's like this. It's no use to belong to two churches. My aunty, you see, still pays my dues at Martin." He says he has lived with many different women, but has never seen fit "to take anybody's daughter to support." He emphasizes the fact that he has never had a venereal disease. It will be noted above, however, that the physical examination showed that he made a four plus Wassermann.

He has led a very unattached, impersonal existence. Even as a boy, while pretending to go to school, he took his lunch up town, shined shoes, and gathered rags. His occupation as "snow" seller caused him to identify himself with the Negro underworld of vice and crime, which, in Martin, was not so notorious as it was in the city of Polk, where he went when he was twelve years old. It seems that he never worked since he left the bootblack stand some sixteen years ago, that he has made a living by selling "coke," that he has been in many cities, and that he has lived with many women and now has a venereal disease. In view of these statements, the court records of this Negro become significant, for it will be noted that he has been charged with practically all the petty offenses which an unmarried Negro is susceptible of being involved in: Assault, assault with deadly weapon, attempted rape, fornication and adultery, violation of health ordinance, vagrancy, gambling, resisting health officers, reckless driving, and larceny. This record comes from Polk, alone. What would be his court record if it could be had for all his ramblings? How many names would he have? He is called "Stall Boy" by his prison associates, because he stalls every one who inquires about him. How much of this story is a "stall boy" story? Perhaps quite a bit of it, but the essential parts are not: the known employment statement, court records, eighteen months across the seas, the woman with whom he lived at 9112 Ash Street, Polk, North Carolina.

Conclusions

Ham Taylor, an illiterate, feeble-minded dope fiend and liquor drinker, suffering with syphilis, is a habitual criminal. His habits of life, which doubtless for the most part are the results rather than the causes of his inefficient equipment, only render him less efficient in terms of social adjustment by aggravating and accentuating those specific deficiencies which were originally the cause of the formation of his harmful habits. The range of charges which have been brought against him seems to indicate that his is the failure of general adjustment, rather than that he purposely or even consciously does those things which are contrary to the regulations of society. His life story, although much of it is a fantasy of his own disordered mind, contains enough facts to illustrate the futility of prevailing methods of penal treatment in dealing with men of his type.

LIFE HISTORY OF BOB JOHNSON

Bob Johnson was born on a rented farm in Patrick County, Virginia, and lived there until he was seven years of age, when his father moved to Pendleton, North Carolina, where he rented again. Bob was the fifteenth and last child. At present (1926), most of his brothers and sisters own homes of their own and are highly respected people in the various communities where they live. Bob, unlike his brothers, when he was fifteen began to roam, coming back home only often enough to get all the money his father and his mother had saved. When he was twenty-one, he married and went to live in Pendleton. Since marrying, however, as before, he has taken his fling with many women and, since 1921, has been coming into the courts, each time the charge being a more serious one. It will be noted below, in his court record, that within one year's time he had been in court on four different charges pertaining to crime against persons and, on Thanksgiving Day in 1923, while in a drunken condition, he shot and killed another Negro. He left the city, but was captured within a few hours, brought back and jailed, bound over to the Superior Court, tried, and sentenced to serve from four to six years on the county roads.

Court Record

Date	Offense	Judgment
4- 8-21	Grand larceny	Bound over
4-30-21	Larceny	$5.00 and costs
11-27-22	Assault with deadly weapon	$100.00
11-30-23	Carrying concealed weapon	
11-30-23	Assault with intent to kill	Nolle pros
12-19-23	Murder	4-6 years on roads

General Description

Bob Johnson is dark brown, has a narrow, high face and a broad forehead. He is tall and slim and stands erect, and when he walks he has the carriage of a college student rather than that of a syphilitic, feeble-minded, illiterate Negro criminal. He has nothing akin to that "dumb driven look," which characterizes convict population in general. Although he thinks he got too long a sentence, he is not particularly bitter about it and seems quite self-sufficient in so far as needing help of any kind from others is concerned: he is the antithesis of the "white man's Negro."

Physical Condition

Bob Johnson is twenty-eight years of age, weighs 175 pounds and is six feet tall. At the time of his physical examination, in July, 1926, his blood pressure was as follows: systolic 210, diastolic 190. The comment of the examining physician is quoted:

"I wish to call your special attention to Bob Johnson, who has a blood pressure of 210 systolic, 190 diastolic, and a syphilitic sore on his leg; this pathological condition existing after having taken 606 and mercury. He has no other marked clinical symptoms. Ordinarily with 210 systolic blood pressure one would suffer with vertigo or headaches and perhaps attacks of amnesia. You will, also, notice that he still has a one plus Wassermann."

The examination further showed that his heart rate was 80, no murmurs present; skin, eyes, nose, and ears, normal; teeth bad; throat normal; appetite irregular; that he had a restless temperament, but slept well at night.

Mental Status

The psychological examination showed that Bob Johnson, whose chronological age is twenty-eight, has a mental age of six years, ten months, has an I.Q. of 43, and was found to be entirely illiterate.

Family Background

Bob was born on a rented farm in Patrick County, Virginia. When Bob was seven years old the family moved to a rented farm near Pendleton. For fourteen years the Johnson family rented farms from various people in the immediate locality. Bob's mother died when he was twenty-one years of age. At that time, the family was broken up, and his father left the farm and moved to Pendleton to live with Bob and with another son, who had been living there for one year and three years, respectively. For many years before leaving the farm, Bob's father was not able to work because of chronic rheumatism. The cause of the death of Bob's mother was not known. No information in regard to Bob's grandparents was available, except that they were slaves and lived and died in the vicinity of Patrick County, Virginia.

Bob Johnson at Home on the Rented Farm

According to his statement he did not go to school because "the old man" kept him at home to work. From the time he was fifteen, he spent most of the money that his parents made, and it seems, according to statements by former landlords, that Bob did a minimum amount of the work in raising the crop. He was counted "mean" by the white and the colored people in the community where he lived long before he had reached the age of twenty, although the other members of the family were very highly respected.

Present Family Conditions

Bob is the youngest living child of a family of fifteen, ten boys and two girls still living. Two brothers live near Pendleton, both owning their homes. One brother lives near Montaire, having inherited a farm through his wife; another brother owns his house and lot in Pendleton; still another brother lives "down east" and operates a four-mule farm; yet another lives in the west—but could not be located. The two girls live in the mountains near Montaire. One of Bob's brothers went to France and has never returned, while another brother was waylaid and killed in Pendleton some years ago.

Except for one of Bob's brothers, it seems that the family has never been brought into court on criminal charges. This particular brother got on the roads, escaped, and has not been apprehended.

When Bob's father left the farm and joined his sons in Pendleton, he had $483.00 in a bank at Pendleton. Although he had saved this to bury himself, he spent it in an effort to help Bob get out of his latest trouble. Many of Bob's brothers furnished some money too. At present the old man has nothing. Bob's wife works regularly at a tobacco factory for $15.00 per week. Bob stated that he had $1000.00 in the bank when he went to the roads in 1923. But, upon investigation, it appears that instead of having money which his wife and invalid father could use while he was on the roads, he had used, in an effort to help himself, the entire resources of his family. Bob's wife and father occupy half of a four-room house facing the railroad in Pendleton and manage to live on the wages she earns in the factory.

Bob in the City

When Bob got to Pendleton, at the age of twenty-one, he began working in a tobacco warehouse. His first employer, who has employed him at irregular intervals for several years, during the tobacco sale season, stated that he was an exceptionally good worker, especially when he first came into town from the farm. In addition to working at the tobacco warehouses, he has driven a truck for a local transfer company and has operated a small concrete mixer for a local construction company. Most of his jobs have paid rather well, the tobacco warehouse and transfer company paying a little above manual labor wages, while he received $160 per month during the short time that he operated the concrete mixer.

Soon after Bob arrived in the city he got married. Before and after his marriage he lived with several women, so he stated; he went on to say that he and his wife had never been separated and that he had never stayed away from her more than a month at a time. He seemed to think that he had done quite well.

Two children were born to Bob and his wife, both dying in infancy. It is doubtless true that he had syphilis at that time, for the facts brought out in his medical examination indicate a long standing diseased condition.

Bob lived in a typical Negro neighborhood of the newer type. The houses, although close together and built of cheap material, are comparatively new. These houses from a distant hill look like so many beehives. The streets are not paved, electric lights are not too plentiful, but in spite of these conditions the district is much better than many other Negro neighborhoods in Pendleton.

Bob belongs to no church. He has life insurance with the Cloverleaf Insurance Company, and his wife keeps paid the weekly premiums amounting to 18 cents. From all reports, it seems that Bob's chief amusement in the city has been his drunken brawls, affairs with women, and fights.

Bob as a Convict—A Murderer

Bob is in no wise bitter, but he does think that he got on the roads unjustly, or at any rate for too long a sentence. It is true that he killed another Negro, but this he claims was done in self-defense. According to his story, which upon investigation seems true, it happened like this:—A great number of Negroes were in one of the local Negro retail establishments. Bob was there with the others. About nine o'clock in the evening, a Negro, much drunker than the rest, came in from the street. As he staggered about, he bumped into first one and then another. When he fell against Bob, he laughed hysterically and began to punch Bob in the sides. At first, this "monkey play" amused him, but as the drunken man kept up his silly antics Bob got tired of it and warned him to "stay off." Although the drunken man seemed to resent this, he went staggering out of the room without saying a word. No sooner was he gone than the usual turmoil of talking and laughing set in. This did not last long, however, for within ten minutes the drunken man returned. This time, he was standing in the door with an army rifle in his hand. Bob realized at once that the man was most likely looking for him, so rather than take any chances he leveled his pistol on him and fired. Bob stated that he hated to shoot a man when he was drunk and crazy. When the man fell in the doorway, Bob jumped over his quivering body and escaped. He was captured within a few hours, jailed, tried for murder in the second degree, and sentenced to the roads for a period of 4 to 6 years, to be determined by his conduct at the road camp.

Soon after Bob got to the convict camp, the road superintendent taught him to operate a small concrete mixer. Bob was chosen for the particular work because his long sentence would justify teaching him. At present, Bob is very highly spoken of by the man in charge of the road building crew. He is also highly respected by his fellow Negro prisoners. He does the most skillful work of any person on the job, and he does it so well that the superintendent stated that the county could afford to pay him as much as $160 per month if he were paroled.

Conclusions

The fact that Bob was the youngest child, and his older brothers and sisters left home as he grew up, and that his father was chronically ill made it easier for him to have his own way. Being of good appearance, and quite active, he could easily make his way into the social life of the rural or urban neighborhood. The death of his two children left him quite free to lead a promiscuous and unattached life. As a result of his participation in drunken brawls, at which fights occurred, he was brought before the courts and was put on the county roads. In spite of his mental and physical condition, he is doing a skilled type of work and is doing it so well that the county officials speak as though they will hire him when he has finished his sentence.

His syphilitic condition accompanied by high blood pressure and resulting emotional tension are perhaps an important factor in his career of crime. His criminal record shows that he was before the courts four times for crimes against persons within the year previous to his sentence to the roads. Apparently no effort was made to diagnose his condition and give him medical treatment when he first came to the attention of the courts. Neither were any efforts made through probation or through the service of any constructive social agency to prevent this feeble-minded Negro from continuing his drunken brawls which finally led to his conviction as a murderer.

Chapter X

COUNTY VERSUS STATE CONTROL OF
CONVICT ROAD WORK

IN THIS study of the county chain gang there has been brought forth much evidence of its failure as a penal institution. It is certainly a doubtful economic asset for any county and no one claims for it any great efficiency in building up the character of men convicted of crime. Nevertheless, road work for convicts possesses many advantages, especially in this southern climate, and it should not be condemned entirely because the county chain gang system is open to such serious criticism. Perhaps the chief difficulty has been its method of organization and administration. What possibility is there of reorganizing county convict road work in such a manner that modern standards of penal treatment can be maintained and at the same time the institution be placed on a secure economic basis?

As long as all types of criminals are committed to these road camps without any effort to classify these prisoners into different grades and supply them with work suitable for each group, the evils that have become associated with the chain gang seem inevitable. Work in the open facilitates escapes and, therefore, is not appropriate for desperate men ready to seize any opportunity to break their prison bonds. It has been the presence of such men in these camps that has led to the use of chains and given apparent justification to the maintenance of harsh discipline. The failure to provide separate camps for the more dangerous and desperate men where they could be given work in rock quarries enclosed by strong stockades is largely responsible for the disrepute into which convict road work has fallen in the South. The acceptance of the principle that work on the roads is suitable only for honor men or for those who cán be trusted to remain at their tasks with a minimum of guarding would place convict road work in this state on a new basis and would go far toward eliminating some of its more objectionable features.

In any evaluation of county convict road work as a penal method it must be borne in mind that it originated primarily as a device to make profitable use of the labor of prisoners with a minimum expenditure for buildings and equipment. The idea of reformation was far in the background and still apparently is not thought of as one of the purposes of this method of penal treatment. No one expects the prisoners to leave the chain gang improved in character or better prepared for citizenship. In so far as this institution is supposed to lower the crime rate, this must be accomplished by making the punishment so severe that it will have a deterrent effect on those disposed to commit crimes. For this reason it is difficult to arouse public opinion concerning the evil conditions that are found in many of the convict camps. After all, it is argued, the prisoner is being punished, and society can best be protected against criminality by making the punishment severe. The chain gang was a logical outgrowth of the deterrent philosophy of punishment and continues today in popular favor because this philosophy still dominates the thinking of the mass of people. As long as the institution is believed to be economically profitable to the county governments that maintain it, few questions are raised concerning its methods of administration and its effect on the prisoners themselves. Reports of the State Sanitary Inspector and the State Board of Charities and Public Welfare concerning bad sanitary conditions and brutal treatment by the camp officials are frequently received with indifference or are countered by protests against the policy of molly-coddling prisoners.

This attitude it is true runs through our entire system of administration of criminal justice, but in the chain gang because of its very nature it finds its most complete opportunity for expression. Convict road work as it has been carried on in North Carolina has only in slight measure been influenced by modern developments in the field of penal treatment. With but one type of work available there is no opportunity for vocational education or for the development of skill in any of the trades. The long work day and crowded living quarters make impracticable any classes for the instruction of illiterates or others who might wish to improve their general education. The prevailing methods of management and lack of facilities cut off the prisoners from the wholesome recreation that is generally provided in state prisons. No chaplains are assigned to the county camps and in many cases no provision is made for regular religious services. The small number of prisoners interferes with any plan to segregate them into groups according to race, age, or degree of criminality. In fact it is in many

counties thought impracticable or at least unnecessary to segregate those venereally diseased. The
more desperate and hardened criminals mingle
freely with the young and petty offenders and make
inevitable the harsh measures of restraint characteristic of the chain gang. The administration of
the convict camps tends to get mixed up with
county politics with the result that their management frequently falls into incompetent hands, and
in no case is thought of as a technical job requiring
skill and training.

As long as county convict road work in this state
is characterized by such defects, no convincing ar-
guments can be advanced in justification of its continuance as a penal institution. Fortunately during the past few years there has been real progress
in overcoming the worst abuses of the traditional
chain gang, as is seen in the erection of modern
prisons, the more limited use of shackles and guns,
and greater attention to the welfare of prisoners.
Nevertheless, it is quite apparent that even after
all these improvements have been made, the essential features of the old system still remain. In
many counties flogging remains the chief means of
enforcing discipline. In a majority of the camps
the rudely constructed buildings make it difficult
to observe.even the more elementary rules of sanitation. Records of social statistics of any kind in
connection with the prisoners very rarely exist. In
no county has it seemed practicable to classify the
prisoners and segregate each group into separate
camps with road work assigned only to those capable of working with a considerable measure of freedom. Nothing short of the adoption of this funda-

mental change in policy will make possible the elimination of the evils inherent in this outworn method of penal servitude.

From the point of view of economic efficiency it has been shown in the chapter on the economic aspect of the county chain gang system that in this respect there is much to be desired. The almost universal absence of adequate records makes it impossible to arrive at any definite and final conclusions concerning the economic value of convict labor. The very absence of such records, however, is evidence of business methods that do not make for success. The primitive pick and shovel method of work which still remains the characteristic form of labor in these convict camps, because it is the most suitable form of work for "gunmen," can hardly hope, even with unpaid labor, to compete with modern road building machinery.

This indictment of the county chain gang system is by no means an indictment of the plan of utilizing convict labor for the improvement of public highways. Without doubt road work under the climatic conditions prevailing in the South is healthful and well suited to the capacities of the large group of prisoners accustomed only to unskilled labor. Work must be provided for convicts, and at this time when there is so much emphasis on road building, there is no reason why selected groups of prisoners should not be employed in work of this kind. The important thing is to devise a plan of administration that will insure both economic efficiency and the fundamental purposes for which the prison system has been established.

In a rural state where there are only a few counties with a city of 40,000 population, it is quite apparent that the county unit is too small to maintain a well-equipped system of penal institutions designed for different grades of prisoners. No county convict camp in the state has as many as 200 prisoners at any one time, and in the majority of the county camps forty or fifty is the maximum number. Under such circumstances the best that can be done is to maintain a single type of prison adapted as far as possible to the needs of the majority of the convicts. There must be a larger administrative unit capable of maintaining a prison population of at least 500 before diversified treatment can be economically practicable. One solution of this problem would be a district plan of operation which would automatically eliminate the smaller county camps where frequently the worst conditions are found. Fortunately a legal basis exists for such a district plan in the state law which permits two or more counties jointly to make provision for working convicts on the public roads. [5] Thus far, instead of putting the law into effect, many of the counties have preferred to accomplish a similar purpose under the authority of local laws which enable them to arrange for convicts to work out their road sentences in neighboring counties where convict camps are maintained. When this is done the county receiving the prisoners pays the court costs and then has the right to their labor during their period of imprisonment. At the present time about half of the counties in the state turn over

[5] *Consolidated Statutes of North Carolina*, 1359.

their prisoners to other counties, instead of maintaining convict camps of their own. For several years the convict camp of Buncombe County at Asheville has served as a district prison for all persons sentenced to the roads in the extreme western part of the state. In other parts of the state this assignment of prisoners to other counties takes place in a hit-and-miss manner with no effort to build up district camps advantageously located. If a properly planned district system could be developed, five or six large prison plants would be sufficient for the 2,500 county prisoners now distributed unequally among about 50 counties.

It seems that the present trend is in this direction since many counties are becoming more dissatisfied with their chain gang as it is now operated. Perhaps in this way the small county convict camp will gradually disappear and its place be taken by better equipped prisons maintained by a few counties that desire to employ convict labor. Institutions of this kind would be large enough to provide the diversified forms of labor required by a modern prison system. The convicts adapted to road work and capable of being trusted outside of prison walls could be placed in honor camps located wherever their labor was needed in highway maintenance or construction. Those likely to give trouble when worked in the open could be assigned to the construction of road materials or the repair of road machinery, which could be done behind strong stockades and walls, thus eliminating the need of guns and shackles. A plan of this kind would at once remove much of the stigma which is now associated with convict road work. Assignment to the honor camps would be a goal to be striven for and could be given as a reward for good conduct and for evidence of improvement in character. With convict road work administered in this manner its economic value would be unquestioned and its effect on the prisoners would be uplifting instead of humiliating and degrading.

As evidence of the increasing interest in the maintenance of honor camps, there may be cited the example of several counties, notably Moore, Lee, and Chatham, which have adopted the principle of operating their convict road work on this basis. The county that desires to work only honor men sends the prisoners who it is believed cannot be made trusties to a county where the chain gang system is in operation. In some cases the group of trusties is enlarged by the device of requiring prisoners well known in the county to give bond as a guarantee against their escape. These honor camps have thus far been limited to predominantly rural counties where the prisoners are few in number and are usually local people who would rather serve out their sentence than to be permanently banished from their families and home community. Convict camps of this type in their equipment and management very much resemble those employing free labor and sometimes include regularly employed men as a part of their working force. Both groups of men work on the same basis with the exception that the convicts receive no pay for their work. A great deal of humaneness usually characterizes the management of these camps, and generally accepted traditions in handling prisoners may even be violated by permitting some of the prisoners to spend Sunday at home with their families. One of these convict camps seen on a Sunday afternoon in the course of this investigation presented the unusual picture of families visiting freely with their husbands and sons, some using a neighboring schoolhouse as the place of meeting while others wandered off through the woods. Honor camps of this kind have gone a great distance from the older ideas of severe and degrading punishment, and demonstrate what can be done by counties under existing laws in the improvement of convict road work.

While the plan of establishing district convict camps is a decided improvement over the present method of operation, there are many who believe that the only logical solution of the whole problem is state control of all prisoners. The district plan as above outlined still remains under county management, and presumably would not be continued by any county unless it could be made financially profitable. No county would be willing to tax its citizens in order to bring about the reformation of convicts from other counties. The county prisons established on a district basis would therefore tend to place emphasis upon financial profits rather than upon reformatory methods. The development of such a plan would be an improvement over the present practice, but in the long run might retard the advance of more progressive measures of penal reform.

The principle of state responsibility for the management of all penal institutions seems especially applicable to a state where there are no large urban centers capable of maintaining well-equipped prisons for their own criminal population. The most serious objection to the adoption of this policy in North Carolina is the failure of the state authorities to build up a state prison system in accord with the most approved principles of penal administration. In spite of improvements made in recent years, the management of the state prison has not been removed from political influence; its central building at Raleigh is an out-of-date structure, ill adapted for the proper housing of prisoners; no alienist or psycho-pathologist is on the staff of the prison; and little effort is made on the basis of scientific study to classify the prisoners and provide the sort of treatment required by each group. On the whole, the standards maintained by the state prison are not superior to those found in the best county convict camps. Under present conditions the transfer of county prisoners to state control would be a gain from the point of view of centralizing responsibility, but might not lead immediately to a reorganization of the convict road work on a more efficient basis.

Nevertheless, if the principle of state control of prisoners is sound, there is no special advantage to be secured by delay in abolishing the county chain gang. Perhaps the increased responsibility thrown on the state prison management would be a good means of bringing about the changes in administrative policy and methods that have long been needed. Certainly the adoption of a plan of this far-reaching nature would create a crisis in state penal affairs that should serve to mobilize intelligent public opinion and compel adjustments necessary to meet the new situation. In many ways recent developments at the state prison have been in the line of progress and give encouragement to those who want the state to lead in its efficient treatment of those convicted of crime. The state prison system maintains two large well-equipped farms capable of providing healthful out-door employment to large numbers of prisoners. Road camps have been established in different parts of the state and groups of honor prisoners have been employed by contractors who are engaged in the construction of state highways. A ward has been established for tubercular prisoners at the state tuberculosis sanatorium. Facilities for housing insane prisoners have been provided at the state hospitals for the insane. Additional industries have been introduced into the central prison at Raleigh, so as to give suitable opportunity for employment to different types and grades of prisoners. This trend in the direction of an improved prison system is being accelerated by a growing consciousness of the importance of this problem and must lead inevitably to such further improvements as the remodeling of the prison at Raleigh for use as a central receiving station, the employment of a staff of scientifically trained men to aid in the classification of the prisoners and give the medical treatment needed to cure mental and physical defects, the establishment of a farm colony for women offenders, [6] and the removal of undue political influence from the management of the state prison.

There is good reason for optimism on the part of those who are endeavoring to build up in this state

---

[6] Since this was written the General Assembly has provided for the establishment of such a farm colony for women. *N. C. Public Laws of 1927*, Chapter 219.

a prison system in accord with the most approved principles of modern penology. One of the first steps necessary is the abolition of the county chain gang system, a step already taken by two Southern states, Virginia and Maryland. The continuation of this medieval method of handling criminals is out of harmony with the distinctive advances made by North Carolina in the solution of other important problems. A recent governor of this state, T. W. Bickett, who was tireless in his efforts to improve the penal system and promote public welfare, well expressed the opinion of many thoughtful students of this problem in these incisive words: "As for the county chain gang system, it is hopeless. The only thing to do is to cut off its head."

BIBLIOGRAPHY

Alabama, Legislative Investigating Committee on Convicts and Highways, Report, *Legislative Document*, No. 6, 1919.

Alabama, Prison Inspector, *Report 1922-1924*, "Birmingham, County Convict Camps," pp. 217-221.

American City Magazine, May, 1917, pp. 483-484.

American City Magazine (Town and County Edition), "The Arizona Convict Labor System," February 1920, pp. 99-101.

American Highway Association, *Official Good Roads Yearbook*, 1915, Washington, D. C.

Asher, Joe, "County Road Camps in Arkansas," *Annals American Academy Political and Social Science*, Vol. 46, March 1913.

Barrows, S. J., "Convict Road Building," *Charities*, Vol. 21, pp. 453.

Beasley, R. F., *The Management of Prisoners*, North Carolina State Board of Charities and Public Welfare, 1918, 15 pp.

Beckett, Mrs. A. T., "Road Work for Prisoners in Salem County, New Jersey," American Prison Association, *Proceedings of Congress*, 1919, p. 172.

Bryant, W. K., "Outdoor Work in Michigan," *Annals American Academy of Political and Social Science*, Vol. 46, p. 95.

Clark, Walter, *Is Flogging Legal?* Opinion in *State vs. Mincher*, (Reprint from 90 S. E. p. 431), 1916.

Cocke, W. F., "Convicts on Highways in Florida," *American City Magazine* (Town and County Edition), July 1919, pp. 13-15.

Coleman, G. P., "Convict Labor for Highway Work," *American City Magazine* (Town and County Edition), January 1916, Vol. 14, p. 57.

Coleman, G. P., "Methods and Costs of Employing Convict Labor on Virginia Road Work," *Good Roads*, April 28, 1917, N. S., Vol. 13, pp. 250-255.

"Convict Built Roads Near Denver," *Outlook*, May 24, 1916, Vol. 113, pp. 164-167.

"Convict Camps in the South," National Conference for Social Work, *Proceedings*, 1915, p. 378.

"Convict Labor in 1923," *Monthly Labor Review*, Vol. 18, p. 699.

"Convict Labor on Highway Construction" (in Arizona), *Engineering and Contracting*, December, 1916, Vol. 46, pp. 505-506.

"Convict Labor on Highways Good Business," *Good Roads*, July 30, 1919, N. S., Vol. 18, pp. 65-67.

"Convict Labor on New Jersey State Highways," *Concrete Highway Magazine*, February 1919, Vol. 3, pp. 44-45.

"Convict Labor on Road Construction (in Maine), *Engineering and Contracting*, December 6, 1916, Vol. 46, pp. 507-508.

"Convict Labor on Road Work," *Municipal Journal*, April 5, 1917, Vol. 42, pp. 174-175.

"Convicts on Road Work," *Municipal Journal*, August 2, 1919, Vol. 47, pp. 64-67.

Davis, J. F., "Prison Labor on Works of Public Improvement," Iowa Board of Control, *Bulletin*, January 1916, Vol. 18.

Dodge, Martin,"Government Coöperation in Object Lesson Road Work, *Yearbook*, United States Department of Agriculture, 1901, pp. 409-414.

Dowd, Jerome, *The Negro in American Life*, N. Y., The Century Co., 1926, p. 611.

Fairbanks, H. S., "Convict Labor for Road Work," *Highway Green Book*, Washington, American Automobile Association, 1920, pp. 416-422.

Fairbanks, H. S., Eastmen, R. H., and Draper, W. F., Report on Experimental Convict Road Camp, Fulton County, Georgia, United States Department of Agriculture, *Bulletin*, 583, 1918, p. 64.

"First Prisoners Are Used on Road Work in Maryland," *Delinquent*, October 1917, Vol. 7, pp. 9-12.

Geyser, O. R., "Good Roads and Convict Labor," American Academy of Political Science, *Proceedings*, Vol. IV, No. 2.

Geyser, O. R., "Making Roads and Men," *Scientific American Supplement*, June 24, 1916, Vol. 81, p. 408.

"Good Roads and Good Men," *Motordom*, March, 1915, Vol. 8, pp. 395-398.

Hart, H. H., *Social Problems of Alabama*, Montgomery, 1918, Russell Sage Foundation, Department of Child Helping, Pamphlet, 87 pp., C. H. 38.

Hart, H. H., "Prison Conditions in the South," American Prison Association, Congress, *Proceedings*, 1919, p. 186.

Henderson, Charles R., *Notes on Outdoor Labor for Convicts*, University of Chicago Press, 1907.

Henderson, Charles R., *Penal and Reformatory Institutions*, New York, Russell Sage Foundation, 1910, pp. 68-88.

Hewes, L. I., "The Employment of prisoners in Road Building," American Prison Association, Congress, *Proceedings*, 1916, pp. 410-422.

Hiller, E. T., "Development of the System of Convict Labor in the United States," *Journal of Criminal Law and Criminology*, Vol. 5, June 1914, pp. 241-269.

Holmes, J. A., *Improvement of Public Roads in North Carolina*, Washington, Government Printing Office, 1895, Reprinted from *Yearbook*, United States Department of Agriculture, 1894, pp. 513-520.

Holmes, J. A., "Road Building with Convict Labor in the Southern States," *Yearbook*, United States Department of Agriculture, 1901, pp. 319-32.

"Honor Camps in Iowa and Colorado," *Scientific American Supplement*, June 24, 1916, p. 408.

"Impressions of the Labor Camps of Florida," *Survey*, Vol. 34, p. 103.

"Improvement of the Road System in Georgia," United States Department of Agriculture, *Bulletin*, No. 3.

Jaffrey, Julia K., Editor, *The Prison and the Prisoner*, Boston, Little, Brown and Company, 1917, 216 pp.

Johnson, George E., "Convicts on Nebraska Roads," *American City Magazine*, (Town and County Edition), May 1917, Vol. 16, pp. 483-484.

Johnson, Kate Burr, "North Carolina's Prison System," American Prison Association, *Proceedings of Congress*, 1923, p. 197.

Keller, W. S., "Working Convicts on the Public Roads of Alabama," Alabama, State Highway Department, *Bulletin*, No. 9, 1915, p. 11.

"Louisiana's Convicts," *Independent*, 1899, p. 362.

McConnell, B. M., "Barbarism to Convicts," *Nation*, November 10, 1926, pp. 479-80.

McKelway, A. J., "The Prison System of the Southern States," Henderson, *Penal and Reformatory Institutions*, p. 68.

North Carolina, Board of Charities, *Biennial Report*, 1893-1894.

North Carolina, Board of Charities and Public Welfare, *Biennial Report*, 1920-1922.

North Carolina, Board of Charities and Public Welfare, *Biennial Report*, 1922-24.

North Carolina, Board of Charities and Public Welfare, *Bulletin*, Vol. 6, No. 1.

North Carolina, Board of Health, *Convict Prison Camps, Rules and Regulations Governing Sanitary Management*, 1926, p. 7.

North Carolina, Geologic and Economic Survey, "Economics of Convict Labor in Road Construction," *Good Roads Circular*, No. 97.

North Carolina, Good Roads Association, *Proceedings*, 1902.

North Carolina, State Highway Commission, *Biennial Report*, 1902.

North Carolina State Highway Commission and State Board of Health, *Sanitary and Hygienic Care of Prisoners*, Joint Bulletin, No. 57.

North Carolina, State Prison, *Biennial Report*, 1907-1908.

Ohio, Board of Administration, "Prison Labor for Roads Approved by Twelve States," *Ohio State Institution Journal*, October, 1919, Vol. 2, No. 2, pp. 14-15.

Oliphant, Albert D., *The Evolution of the Penal System of South Carolina from 1866-1916*. Columbia, The State Company, 1916, 14 pp.

"Organization and Administration of Convict Labor Camps, for Highway Work," *American City Magazine*, (Town and County Edition), May, 1919, Vol. 20, pp. 432-434.

"Organization and Equipment of Convict Camps in Georgia; Methods and Cost, *Engineering and Contracting*, March 31, June 2, 1915, Vol. 43, pp. 290-291, 500-502.

Pennypacker, J. E., Fairbank, H. S., Draper, W. F., *Convict Labor for Road Work*, United States Department of Agriculture, Bulletin 414, 1916, 218 pp.

Pratt, Joseph Hyde, "Convict Labor in Highway Construction," *American Academy of Political and Social Science*, Vol. 46, p. 78.

"Prisoners and Good Roads" *Nation*, Vol. 98, April 23, 1914, pp. 453-454.

"Road Construction by Convicts," American Prison Association, Congress 1915, *Proceedings*, p. 32.

"Road Improvement in McDowell County (West Virginia)," *Good Roads*, November 25, 1916, N. S., Vol. 12, pp. 213-214.

"Roadmaking as a reform measure," *Survey*, Vol. 26, April 22, 1911, pp. 157-159.

Roberts, James, *Tennessee, Bushy Mountain Prison and the Southern Chain Gang*, Joplin-Taylor Printing and Publishing Company, (1925).

Saunders, W. O., "Cleaning Out North Carolina's Convict Camps," *Survey*, May 15, 1915, p. 152.

South Carolina, Board of Charities and Corrections, *Annual Reports*, 1915-1919.

South Carolina, Board of Charities and Corrections, *Handbook on Jail, Chain Gang, and Almshouse Management*, Columbia, 1918, 55 pp. (Quarterly Bulletin, Vol. 4, No. 3.)

South Carolina, Board of Charities and Corrections, "How County Jails, Chain Gangs, and Almshouses Measure up to Our Standards," *Quarterly Bulletin*, Vol. 3, No. 2, pp. 52-53.

South Carolina, Board of Charities and Corrections, "The Treatment of Convicts on Some of Our County Chain Gangs," *Quarterly Bulletin*, Vol. 3, No. 1, pp. 31-72.

South Carolina, Board of Public Welfare, *Manual on Chain Gang Management*, 1924, 16 pp.

South Carolina, Board of Public Welfare, *Reports*, 1920-1924.

Stanford, J. L., *Utilization of Short-Term Convicts for Highway Work in Georgia*, New York, National Committee on Prisons and Prison Labor, 1915, 7 pp.

Stovall, D. H., "Boulevards Built by Honor Men," *Sunset*, Vol. 28, pp. 496-498.

Tannenbaum, Frank, *Darker Phases of the South*, New York, G. P. Putnam's Sons, 1924, pp. 74-115

Tompkins, D. A., *Road Building in a Southern State*, Charlotte, Observer Publishing House, 1897, 17 pp.

Tutwiler, Julia S., "Alabama's Prison System," National Conference of Charities and Corrections, *Proceedings*, 1893, p. 29.

Tynan, T. J., "Prison Labor on the Public Roads," *Annals American Academy of Political and Social Science*, Vol. 46, pp. 58-60.

United States, Congress, House, Committee on Judiciary, *To Authorize the Working of Federal Convicts upon Public Highways*, Hearings on H. R. 5772, February 28, March 1, 3, 1916, Washington, 1916, 43 pp. (Serial 1).

United States, Congress, Senate, Discussion of Convict Labor, *Congressional Record*, Vol. 57, February 8, 1919, pp. 2971-2972.

United States, Commissioner of Labor, *Convict Labor*, Annual Report, 1886, 612 pp.

United States, Department of Agriculture, *Notes on the Employment of Convicts in Connection with Road Building*, Bulletin No. 16 (Revised).

United States, Department of Labor, Bureau of Labor Statistics, *Convict Labor in 1923*, Washington, 1925, (Bulletin No. 372), 265 pp.

"Value of Convict Labor," *American City Magazine*, Vol. 24, 1921, p. 20.

Warren, George C., "Convict Labor on County Roads," *Municipal Engineering*, Vol. 48, pp. 26-33.

Weyland, Lorenzo D., *A Study of Wage-payment to Prisoners as a Penal Method*, (Chicago, 1920) 106 pp. (Reprint from *Journal of Criminal Law and Criminology*, Vol. 10, No. 4, Vol. 11, Nos. 1, 2, February, May, August, 1920).

Williams G. Croft, *Crime and its Treatment in South Carolina*, Columbia, 1922, 16 pp. (State Board of Public Welfare Bulletin, Vol. 3, No. 2).

Williams, S. M., "The Honor System in the Use of Prison Labor for Road Construction, *American City Magazine*, (Town and County Edition), Vol. 17, November 1917, pp. 395-398.

Wilson, P. St. Julien, "Convict Camps in the South," National Conference of Charities and Corrections, *Proceedings*, 1915, pp. 378-385.

DISTRIBUTION OF COUNTY CHAIN GANGS IN NORTH CAROLINA
County or township convict road camps are found in shaded counties